Words Matter

by

Robert Byrum

The contents of this work, including, but not limited to, the accuracy of events, people, and places depicted; opinions expressed; permission to use previously published materials included; and any advice given or actions advocated are solely the responsibility of the author, who assumes all liability for said work and indemnifies the publisher against any claims stemming from publication of the work.

All Rights Reserved
Copyright © 2021 by Robert Byrum

No part of this book may be reproduced or transmitted, downloaded, distributed, reverse engineered, or stored in or introduced into any information storage and retrieval system, in any form or by any means, including photocopying and recording, whether electronic or mechanical, now known or hereinafter invented without permission in writing from the publisher.

Dorrance Publishing Co
585 Alpha Drive
Pittsburgh, PA 15238
Visit our website at *www.dorrancebookstore.com*

ISBN: 978-1-6386-7155-8
eISBN: 978-1-6386-7688-1

Words Matter: by Robert Byrum

"Words have meaning; words without sincerity have no meaning; truth has meaning; words without truth have no meaning. Work and effort have meaning; work without effort has no meaning. True friends have meaning; false friends aren't worth bothering about." Author Unknown

Sometime in the many years past I started collecting short stories, quips, and sayings of wisdom, intelligence and humor. Then it grew into writing about subjects I felt were thought provoking and enduring. Eventually I had a computer library crammed with a wide variety of subjects standing by themselves with no place to go. My desire is that those thoughts included in this book will find a home and be useful to others that share a willingness to reflect on the business of living, of life, love, to cherish their lives, some chuckles and maybe a few tears. My hope is that they will be received and enjoyed with that in mind.

Anticipation:
"Our lives hold a vail between anticipation and horror. Anticipation is the carrot suspended before the jack- ass to keep him moving forward. Horror is what he would see if he took his eyes off the carrot."

– Louis L'Amour

What is it? Has anyone really asked? It is more than just a Webster's definition. It is the very soul of life, the bread we feed on. Some may call it foresight or dreaming but it is much more than just a wish. It is the core that has driven us since our mother's womb. Did we anticipate and seek nourishment before birth? Is anticipation just a conscience act or is it part of our inner self, part of our individual makeup and a vital element in our ability to exist as a functional human being? Is it living in the conciseness of the present moment?

How often do we think of its meaning and significance in our daily lives? To live we cannot exist in a void of suspended thought, there has to a purpose and direction. One higher level of this is something within us we call anticipation. It defines our living experience and our safety. Is anticipation stronger in our youth and do we grow dull to its influence as we grow older? The excitement of a child waiting for Santa, the ice cream cone, the first date, the first car, we call this youthful enthusiasm. Enthusiasm is the engine started by anticipation.

We must anticipate to be happy, to be sad, to be frightened and to achieve something meaningful. It is not always pleasant; it is not dreaming or wishful thinking. How does it differ from these simplifications? It covers the complete emotional core of our being: happiness, sadness and the future of our lives: it is with us tomorrow, next week, next month or the next minute. It is our protector and our comforter and without it we would not be alert to danger or pleasure. If we don't listen to it carefully, we may fall on an icy sidewalk, wreck our car or worse. It has protected us all of our lives. Our minds control all of its functions either consciously or sub- consciously or as often in that gray area that occurs somewhere in between.

To anticipate is to exist. Our individual interest and experiences direct the ebb and flow of our anticipation. No two people experience the same effects of this emotion, even considering the subject and in the same time frame, we differ. Why? Do we draw on past experiences to form today's predictions, actions or reactions? Sure. How valid are our anticipated thoughts? Do we fool ourselves? Absolutely, for the very act is one of mystery. If we could would we dare push it out of our being? Only at the price of our own safety, our happiness, our inner peace and yes, our frustrations.

As I write this, I am setting on a large rock overlooking a beautiful lake in the far northern Canadian wilderness; in the distance a pair of Common Loons surface and call their haunting melody. A large dragon fly lands on my leg to say hello. Does he anticipate and if he does not, how does he avoid the reeds and willows he so artfully flies through? A horse fly just bit me; did he anticipate the meal? I suspect he did not anticipate getting slapped as he lays at my feet. I have missed more than I have hit, maybe the smart ones anticipate. Do the loons anticipate their next fish?

In an hour I will go fishing and I contemplate why I fish. What is it that makes fishing addictive, what will the next few hours bring? Anticipation of the unknown and also of the possible: a fish, how big, what species? Danger, yes, I will be out in a boat by myself on a strange lake that should always be a cause for concern. Fear a little for a fool is without fear. But to anticipate too much fear; no, I must guard against that for to be too cautious is to limit living. We can be too cautious right up to the grave but we will still be dead and consider what we have missed. A balance should be sought in all things.

But again, why do I fish? To be on the water, relaxed and enjoying the scenery? This morning I saw a moose and a mink, what will I see this evening? It is the unknown of what the next cast will bring: what size, what species and what will appear around the bend of the next little island? We can anticipate the unknown, what if we could not? The mechanics of catching fish are fun but not my only reason for being here. It is the unknown; the expectation that's drives me, without these life and fishing would be pretty dull.

Henry David Thoreau said" A man goes fishing all his life and does not realize it's not the fish he is after." That pretty much sums it up. It is the experience we are seeking.

As I write I am anticipating the near future. What of the intermediate future? Going home, the long drive, the welcome of my wife and my labs, seeing the garden and how its grown. And the distant future, it is wise not to dwell too much on this; direct expectations to the near horizon.

Driving home from this remote wilderness with its beauty of lakes and forests I think of the coming change and have mixed feelings. How refreshing these last few days were on that little island, where the senses were directed to the beauty of nature and simple thoughts. Anticipation is a learning process; we must adjust our thoughts and actions constantly to our surroundings. As we drive, we should be aware of all the conditions that might occur at any moment. At present I think of a moose that could suddenly appear on the road or that semi-truck that just passed hauling a load of hay. What would I do if he blew a tire or lost his load? Where would I steer to avoid the moose? This is not doomsday thinking but instant awareness, a valuable self-preservation tool that must be nurtured. It is living and staying in the moment.

Anticipation means action. We must take certain actions to satisfy our anticipation. The gardener must prepare the soil and plant to fulfill his anticipation of the beauty that will occur.
It also means sacrifice, for a secure future we must sacrifice some of the pleasures of today to obtain an education, to see our children graduate and to secure a rewarded healthy retirement.

As I get older it seems to take more effort to appreciate anticipation. Maybe it's the "been there done that" syndrome. We must guard against this with all our strength for if we lose the thrill, the caution the pain and frustration we lose the core of our being. New experiences, travel, new peoples and different thoughts create a big chunk of what it means to anticipate and to be alive.

"Write it in your heart that every day is the best day of the year. No man has learned anything rightly, until he knows that every day is Doomsday."
    – Ralph Waldo Emerson

Jokes and Serious Stuff

   How do you know when you're getting older?
   Everything hurts and what doesn't hurt doesn't work.

The gleam in your eye is from the sun hitting your glasses.

You feel like the night before and you haven't been anywhere.

Your little black book contains only the names ending in MD.

You get winded playing chess.

Your children began to look middle aged.

You finally reach the top of the ladder and find its leaning against the wrong wall.

You join a health club and don't go.

You decide to procrastinate, but never get around to it.

Your mind makes contracts that your body can't meet.

You know the answers but nobody asks you the questions.

You look forward to a dull evening.

You walk with your head held high trying to get used to the tri-focals.

You set in a rocking chair and can't get it going.

Your knees buckle but your belt wont.

Dialing long distance wears you out.

The best part of your day is when the alarm clock goes off.

Your back goes out more than you do.

A fortune teller offers to read your face.

The little gray-haired lady you help across the street is your wife.

Love:

"For as love is often won with beauty so it is not kept preserved and continued but by virtue and obedience."

– Utopia by Thomas Moore

As we use this word today what does it project to us? Historically it has been a word that has been meant to convey a sincere positive emotional reaction to another person. It is another word that has been brutalized in our language. Has its significance been misused and lessoned to the point that it now has a diminishing effect on us?

Great scholars, composers and poets down through the ages have used "love" in many wonderful works; plays, songs and poetry to capture and express its meaning. They could make music out of words. And when we are fortunate to experience these works our emotions are aroused and we feel something.

Do we experience these same emotions today when we hear such expressions as: I love ice cream, isn't this a lovely day or I love my new hat? Do we really? Do we dimmish its effects and response by repeating and hearing these shallow expressions every day? Do we convey to others from our habit of hearing them, a lack of emotion when we tell our wife and children that we love them when the word has been overused and it no longer conveys personal affection and tenderness? Do we lessen its sincerity by such use when we use it to be sincere?

"If you'd be loved, be worthy of love."
    – Ovid

"Love many things, for therein lies the true strength, and whosoever loves much performs much, and can accomplish much, and what is done in love is well done.
    – Vincent van Gogh

"Love for the joy of loving, and not for the offerings of someone else's heart."
    – Marlene Dietrich

"Treasure each other in the recognition that we do not know how long we shall have each other."
    – Joshua Liebman

"True love comes quietly, without banners or flashing lights. If you hear bells, get your ears checked."
    – Erich Segal

"Keep love in your heart. A life without it is like a sunless garden when the flowers are dead. The consciousness of loving and being loved brings warmth and richness to life that nothing else can bring."
– Oscar Wilde

"You must love that all that God has created, both his entire world and each single tiny sand grain of it. Love each tiny leaf, each beam of sunshine. You must love the animals, love each plant. If you love all things, you will also attain the divine mystery that is in all things. For then your ability to perceive the truth will grow every day, and your mind will open itself to an all-embracing love."
– Fyodor Dostoyevsky

Dogs Love:
"Love sought is good but given unsought is better."
– Twelfth Night, William Shakespeare

Dogs don't care if your skin color is black, brown, yellow or multi-colored. Dogs don't care if you are rich, poor, old, young or crippled. Their love is universal and once they love you its complete and everlasting. They express that love openly in many ways every day, it's up to us to recognize and appreciate what they are saying. When you leave them, they show you they are sad and when you return, they are ecstatic with their barking, wining and body wiggles. They are saying "I love you" and in return asking to be loved. They never hold back and never should we, they don't know how. Their emotions are always open, never to be hidden, never phony.

A dog communicates with his eyes; they ask to be fed, to go potty, to tell us when they hurt and certainly to express their affection. Sometimes direct human to dog eye contact is difficult to obtain, maybe it is an inheritance trait because in their wild history it represented a challenge, but once it is archived you have a window into their heart. It is love in its purest form.

Letter to My Son: Author unknown

Dear Son,

Just a few lines to let you know I'm still alive. I'm writing this letter slowly, because I know you cannot read fast. You won't know the house when you come home-we've moved.

About your father-he has a lovely new job. He has 500 men under him He is cutting the grass at the cemetery.

There was a washing machine in the new house when we moved in, but it isn't working too well. Last week I put 14 shirts into it and pulled the chain, and I haven't seen the shirts since.

Your sister Mary had a baby this morning. I haven't found out whether it is a boy or a girl, so I don't know whether you're an aunt or an uncle.

Your Uncle Dick drowned last week in a vat of whisky at the Dublin Brewery. Some of his workman dived in to save him but he fought them off bravely. We cremated his body and it took three days to put out the fire.

I went to the doctor on Thursday, and your farther came with me. The doctor put a tube in my mouth and told me not to open it for ten minutes. Father offered to buy it from him.

It only rained twice last week. First for 3 days and then for 4 days. Monday it was so windy that one of our chickens laid the same egg four times.

We had a letter yesterday from the undertaker. He said if the last installment wasn't paid on your grandmother within 7 days, up she comes.

Your loving Mother

PS I was going to send you ten dollars but I had already sealed the envelope.

There I stood before the mail box with a face so very red, instead of mailing your letter I have opened it instead!

Aging:
"Age isn't just the amount of time passed; it's a state of mind. If you think young and feel young you will be young."

– Unknown author

We experience transitions in life as we move from childhood to our teens; from young adults to middle age and into our senior years. Each step changes us physically and mentally mostly for the better. But as we arrive at being seniors there is sometimes apprehension and fear. A concern that the end of the road is near and as we fret and worry; we help shorten the distance.

When we were young, we never expected that there would be an end. As we grew, life was mostly on the upbeat. We challenged it, we enjoyed and worked hard for the rewards that it gave us, it was positive and fun. Occasionally some disappointments but for the most part it was worth being around.

We had known, but rarely acknowledge that there was end time. Looking to the end time is a way of falling to appreciate the present, the only time that is really ours.

"Dost, thou love life? Then do not squander time; for that is what the stuff life is made of."

– Benjamin Franklin

It's helpful to look at life and ask: "If I had one more year to live, what would I do?" We all have things we want to achieve. Don't just put them off- do them now!

– John Goddard

We have enjoyed life; we have loved and been loved and have experienced many beautiful places and things. We have secured countless memories that we cherish and will always have to relive and share. But now in the ebb tide of our lives we come to a fork in road we must decide which path to take. One sign says "Positive", the other, well we shouldn't even consider that way. We cannot turn now from a lifetime of being optimistic, happy and confident and retreat in despair. Every second, minute, hour and day of life is precious regardless of age. Grab on to it, love, laugh and be contented.

– Byrum

"If you make a life that gives you joy you have no time to get old."
– Henry Winkler

"It's a very short trip. While alive, live!"
– Malcolm Forbes

"Old age must be resisted, and its deficiencies supplied by taking pains; we must fight it as we do disease. Care must be bestowed upon health; moderate exercise should be taken; food and drink should be sufficient to recruit, not overcome our strength. And not the body alone must be sustained, but the powers of the mind much more; unless you supply them, as oil to a lamp, they too grow dim with age. Whereas over ex-exertion weights the body down with fatigue, exercise makes the mind buoyant."
– Marcus Cicero

Do not save your loving speeches
For your friends till they are dead;
Do not wright them on their tombstones,
Speak them rather now instead.
– Anna Cummins

Youth:

"You will make all kinds of mistakes, but as long as you are generous and true, and also fierce, you cannot hurt the world or even seriously distress her. She was made to be wooded and won by youth."

– Winston Churchill

"The secret of staying young is to live honestly, eat slowly, and lie about your age."

– Lucille Ball

On Serious Illness. "It is better to live and be done with it then to die daily in the sickroom. By all means began your folio; even if the doctor does not give you a year, even if he hesitates about a month, make one brave push and see what can be accomplished in a week. Does not life go down with a better grace, foaming in full body over a precipice, than miserably straggling to an end in a sandy delta? For surely, at whatever age it overtakes the man, this is to die young."

– Robert Louis Stevenson

"Don't ever let me catch you singing like that again, without enthusiasm. You're nothing if you aren't excited by what you're doing."

– Frank Sinatra to his son Frank Jr.

"Watch me, learn from me and learn my mistakes."

– Judy Garland's advice to her daughter Liza Minnelli

A way of life from a 96-year-old

>Be aware and happy with what you got. Be active; exercise your body and mind. If you don't use it, you lose it. Don't buy

trouble, look at the good things; get rid of the bad things and go with the people who are positive.

"Face your deficiencies and acknowledge them; but do not let them master you. Let them teach you patience, sweetness, insight. When we do the best, we can, we never know what miracle is wrought in our life, or in the life of another."

– Helen Keller

This God Forsaken Land: From the Madisonian Paper, 1981

This "God Forsaken Land" they call it
As they gaze with pitying eye
Nothing here but hills and sagebrush
And a vast expense of sky

"We don't know how you take it"
Those city folks declare
"And how do you make a living?
Or do live on air?

They wonder at the twinkle in our eye
And the smiles we try to hide
For in all this lonely, windswept land
They see no reason for pride

But we could tell them of our ranches,
Where great herds of cattle roam
And the flocks of bleeping woolies
That claim Montana home

We could show them our oil wells
That pour forth liquid gold
And in those places, they call "barren"
There are deep, rich veins of coal

They may not see our fertile ranches
With fields of hay and grain
But nestled there among the hills
We have them just the same

To the "loneliness" they talk about
To us is Gods own peace
There's so much beauty all around
That our thanks shall never cease

Our streams are filled with trout
We've antelope, elk and deer
Were a mile up nearer heaven
And the air is pure and clear

Our sunsets glow with color
And in the pearly dawn of morn
The pungent scent of sage drifts down
On a breeze that's mountain born

We don't know much of city life
Or where they seek God there
But we do know in Montana
That we find him everywhere

So, to them we'll leave the cities
Where the living is so grand
And we'll stay in Montana
In our God- Beloved land

The Mayonnaise Jar: Author unknown

When things in your life see almost too much to handle. When 24 hours in a day is not enough; remember the mayonnaise jar and the 2 cups of coffee.

A professor stood before his philosophy class and had some items in front of him.

When the class began, wordlessly he picked up a very large empty mayonnaise jar and started to fill it with golf balls. He asked the students if the jar was full. They agreed it was.

The professor picked a jar of pebbles and poured it into the jar. He shook the jar lightly. The pebbles rolled into the open areas between the golf balls. He asked the students again if the jar was full. They agreed that it was.

The professor then picked up a box of sand and poured it into the jar. Of course, the sand filled everything else. He asked once more if the jar was full. The students responded with a unanimous "yes."

The professor then produced two cups of coffee from under his desk and poured the contents into the jar, effectively filling the empty space between the sand.

The students laughed." Now" said the professor, as the laughter subsided, "I want you to recognize that this jar represents your life."

The golf balls are the important things, God, family, children, health friends and favorite passions. Things that if everything else was lost and only they remained your life would still be full. The pebbles are the things that matter like your job, house and car.

The sand is everything else, the small stuff. "If you put the sand in the jar first" he continued, there is no room for the pebbles or the golf balls.

The same goes for life. If you spend all your time and energy on the small stuff, you will never have room for the things that are important to you. So- pay attention to the things that are critical to your happiness, play with your children, take the time to get medical checkups, take your partner out to dinner.

There will always be time to clean the house and fix the dripping faucet.

Take care of the golf balls first, the things that really matter. Set your priorities. The rest is just sand. One student inquired what the coffee represent. The professor smiled, "I'm glad you asked."

It goes to show you that no matter how full your life may seem, there's always room for a couple cups of coffee with a friend.

Our Senses: Robert Byrum

"A man needs to milk his hours of the precious things-sunsets, sunrises, a flowing river, a beautiful tree, the love of an animal, so many wonderful things. To ride fast and travel far these were empty things, unless a man took the time to savor, to taste, to listen, to love and simply be."

– Louis L' Amour

It is important to listen to your senses and to feel and be aware, they are the gateway to the present and are your conscious connection to being alive. "To live in the moment," is a phrase we frequently hear today. But what does it mean?

In every human act our senses are a factor. Our minds control these factors and many of them are automatically programmed into our actions. They anticipate our movements, our speech, our emotions but unfortunately in many of our actions we have put our senses switch on automatic and our brains in neutral. As we have lessened our contact with nature, we have diminished her many gifts and become slaves to habit.

To live is not only to exist. To live is to feel, and the senses have much to re -teach us if we pay attention. To be alive is to be aware and to enjoy every day the use of all of our senses.

> We look but we do not see
>
> We hear but we do not listen
>
> We eat but we do not taste
>
> We touch but we do not feel
>
> We speak but we do not listen
>
> We sniff but we do not smell
>
> We read but we do not comprehend
>
> We are aware but we are not curious, we are slow to imagine

Unfortunately, today in our world of wondrous gadgets we are constantly distracted from the use of our natural abilities. Our senses have been dumbed down and we live by reaction and not by perception. We have become mentally and sensually lazy. We have lost the appreciation and efficient use of so many of our senses through neglect. The challenge is to learn and appreciate again what we have always had.

It has been said that our ability to use and appreciate our senses diminish as we grow older. I do not believe that. They are not lost or diminished they are neglected by disuse, bad habits, lack of awareness and laziness. The world of a four-year old child is a wonderous place. They really taste their ice cream cones and their curious questions are without end. Why can't we?

Consider the American Indian. In his natural state he was very perceptive and appreciative of the natural world in which he lived. He observed the environment and lived by his observations. The moon and the sun were his calendar. His sense of smell was always important. The forest, the waters the plants and animals were his existence. In order to survive he had to listen, hear and smell well. He had to see and observe carefully and he had to be curious about the game he hunted and the enemies who hunted him. If lost or abused these abilities he died.

We Look but We Do Not See:

"I who am blind can give one hint to those who see, one admonition to those who would make full use of the gift of sight. Use your eyes as if tomorrow you would be stricken blind. And the same method can be applied to the other senses. Hear the music of voices, the song of a bird, the mighty strains of an orchestra, as if you would be stricken deaf tomorrow. Touch each object you want to touch, as if tomorrow your tactile sense would fail. Smell the perfume of flowers, taste with relish each morsel, as if tomorrow you could never smell and taste again. Make the most of every sense."

– Helen Keller

We look at flowers but do we study the beauty and intricacies of a single one? Pick one and study it carefully. We look at clouds but do we see their many variations, their colors, their shapes and movements? We glance here and there without thought or study. How about rocks, water or people? They are candy for our eyes. When we speak or spoken to, do we gain and maintain eye contact?

Do we look carefully to observe and appreciate the emotions expressed in people's faces; the joy, the sorrow and the questions not spoken? How well do we read people?

Watching people is a fun hobby where our sense of observation can amuse and enlighten our day. We should learn not to see crowds but individuals in their unlimited variations. We all have sat in an airport, sometimes for hours, waiting for a flight, bored to tears while all around us, people, hundreds of our unique species invade our vision. The variation is limitless. For a fun start, observe the variety of shoes. Beautiful ankles sometimes freshen our attention. Then move on to other moving body parts and attachments. Hats, sweaters (for real variety), facial expressions, the list is almost endless. It is a variety show with numerous chuckles that the most skilled comedy producers would be challenged to duplicate. It's all ours for free if we just learn to look.

How recently have you studied a single flower, a tree or a bush? The variations of so many different types, shapes, textures and colors, the intricacies of their structure and their adaptability to their environment are an amazing miracle. Think, what if tomorrow a single flower was discovered on some distant planet? What would be the reaction? The whole world would explode with excitement and we would observe and study its uniqueness. We would see it. It would be the event of the ages. A single flower, and yet here on our speck of earthen dust in the vastness of space we have billions of flowers that few of us rarely see, notice or appreciate.

Clouds; Do we see them or just look at them or do we even look? Yes, it takes time to observe, to appreciate, to wonder and marvel at the limitless variations that occur within our short attention span. When we were young, we would observe clouds and with our youthful imaginations would see faces, objects, animals in their formation. Do we still: can we still: why not?

What would be enjoyment of a blind person who never has seen, suddenly is blessed with the wondrous world of sight? How exciting it is for them to see for the first time the green of a tree; a sunset; a baby's face, the moon and the night sky. Why must we be blinded to appreciate our wonderful world? Why should these pleasures be limited to the cured infirmed? We ourselves are blinded by the habit of looking and not seeing.

Such a simple thing as rocks: An endless verity of color, texture and shape all lying at our feet waiting to be noticed. They seem to say "pick me up look at me, I'm one of a kind" and they are. No two are exactly alike. No two have the same shape, texture, color or chemical composition. They are like snowflakes, not fallen from the heavens but pushed up from the depths of our planet to be broken, washed smooth and polished. And they are permanent at our feet, not fleeting. If one were a diamond or a ruby, we would notice it. They are in their own way diamonds in the rough if we would learn to look.

"The art of leisure lies, to me, in the power of absorbing without effort the spirit of one's surroundings; to look, without speculation, at the sky and sea; to become part of the green plain; to rejoice, with tranquil mind, in the feast of color in a bed of flowers."

– Dian Calthrop

We Hear but Do Not listen

Any wife (or husband) will attest to this. But it is much more than domestic encounters. When was the last time you really listen to the wind or the singing of a bird or the sound of beautiful music or the wave on a beach or a child's happiness? To not hear what is around us is self-isolation.

Anyone, who has lost a portion of their hearing, realizes the moment they insert their hearing aids the world changes and the wonders of sound returns. Correctable hearing loss has an advantage. It teaches us to appreciate. Consider those unfortunate individuals who have never heard the wonders of sound. How would they react if suddenly they were given that miracle? They would be amazed and appreciative at what we take for granted, and they would surely listen.

It is not easy to really listen; you must concentrate and have quite in your mind. It is difficult to find a quiet place anymore. If you find one cherish the experience. Today in our modern world bombarded with continuous noise we must train ourselves to block out all of the background chatter and make a real effort to listen. There is such a thing as the music of silence.

"As long as you live, keep learning how to live."

– Seneca

We Eat but We Do Not Taste

When was the last time you really spent the time really tasting what you were eating? Mom told us to "chew our food." A better advise may have been to chew and taste our food. The two are not the same. We shovel food into our food factory so that it becomes a habit not an experience even for the most delectable things. Next time try really tasting that apple or that steak. Our taste buds are there for the mind to wake them up.

What we do in our hurried life is to chew and swallow with hardly any consideration to taste. We multi-task while we are eating, we gulp like a hungry puppy. Slow down, roll a small bite around in your mouth and swallow small bits, savor it as you swallow. Like all of our senses tasting is a habit born of thought and practice. We must think and practice taste in order to enjoy one of life' greatest pleasures. But to do so we must slow down and chew like Mom said but taste and delight in the experience. Try it.

We Touch but We Do Not Feel

The simple act of touching has become so much of our automatic sensual program that for most of us it is a lost appreciated sense. Our minds control the action of our hands and through them our sense of feel. How many different touch sensations do our fingers transmit instinctually to our minds? Right now, reach out and touch something, anything, then touch something else. Did you notice the difference? Would you have noticed if you hadn't thought about the experience of what you were feeling? Pause a moment and touch something else. Do they feel the same? The verities of touching are endless but how often are we aware of them?

We do think when we pick up that hot cup of coffee, our mind tells us to be careful. When did we learn this, was it the first hot experience? The wind the cold, the heat, the wet, the smooth, the soft and the rough are all part of our sense of feel. Are we as appreciative of them as the blind person? Why not?

We Sniff but We Do Not Smell

Smelling it seems is an automatic response to our senses but we can think to smell. We smell horrible things and try to block out our sense of them. But how often do we appreciate the pleasant smells around us? Smell is linked to our brain area that process emotion and memories so a whiff of anything pleasant can induce pleasure. Try smelling a lilac flower when it is in full bloom. When was it when you stopped to smell not only the roses but the wind, the damp earth after a shower, an ocean breeze, freshly mowed grass, a new puppy, the smoke of a wood fire, an orange, a morsel of food? Or do these and other unlimited pleasant smells of life pass through your nose with hardly a thought?

Again, we put our brain in automatic. We may sniff them as they pass, but do we think about them and let them linger in our consciousness?

We miss so much pleasure by not being aware. How do we use this sense? Can we smell danger? Certainly. Can we experience emotion by smelling? Of course. Stand in a pine forest on a warm evening and our emotions are aroused by their fragrance. Have you smelled the sea on an early morning or a garbage truck passing? What was your reaction to these smells; stimulating, calmness, offensive?

Oh, for the nose of a canine. What would it be like to be able to smell as they do with a sense of smell thousands of times greater than ours? How interesting and exciting it would be. New wonders would appear, not always pleasant but exciting and stimulating.

Each individual's reaction to smell is different and can be condition to our environment. Butchers and fish mongers don't mind the smell, they have been conditioned but a customer's nose may be offended. Our sense of smell is honed and conditioned by our individual life experiences. We can change our reaction and become used to or immured to smells.

We Speak but We Do Not Think or Listen

So much is said and so little is meaningful. Babble is everywhere in our daily lives; it floods us and is unavoidable. It fills our ears with constant noise and little thought or meaning. Where is the Plato's, the Socrates and our Aristotle of today? Will we ever have another? These great minds weren't just born they were developed over time by listening, thinking and then being able to express that great knowledge in simple speech and writing. How much better is it to have more thinking and less noise? If we use the practice of "WAIT" as in "Why am I talking", and slow down as we speak to listen carefully to what we hear before responding it would make for a much calmer life.

Contentment: by Jack Kornfield

If you can sit quietly after difficult news, if in financial downturns you remain preferably calm, if you can see your neighbors travel to fantastic places without a twinge of jealousy, if you happily eat whatever is put on your plate, and fall asleep after a day of running around without a drink or a pill, if you can always find contentment just where you are, you are probably a dog.

This is really contentment, there is so much we can learn from our animal friends.

We Are Aware but We Are Not Curious

The most valuable word that we have is "why". When we were young that was our first expression, we used it to get attention and to understand information. We were born with this appetite to know and we wanted to know it now: "why mommy", "why", "why". "Whys" were a big part of our young vocabularies and often times, unfortunately, they were discouraged with "because I said so" or "that's just the way it is" or other small put-downs that eventually discouraged the asking and we quit. Those who were encouraged to keep asking and got patient explanations were fortunate for that one word could lead to a life of curiosity and the appreciation and inventions of so many things and wonderful accomplishments. It is one of the foundations of learning and of great achievements for mankind, from that single word.

"A patient pursuit of the facts (why), and a cautious combination and comparison of them is a drudgery to which man is subjected by his maker, if he wishes to obtain sure knowledge."

– Thomas Jefferson

To be curious is to be alive and informed; to not be easily fooled nor to except things at first glance but to ask, "why?" To question ourselves and others and what is happening to the world around us. Our curiosity has gone astray. We are fed "facts" and "truths" through the various media and fail to question with the "why's" that are necessary to be fully and correctly, honestly informed. It is easier that way then to have to think, investigate and compare; but we can be curious again by just asking "why." Why not?

We Are Slow to Imagine

Imagination: what a wonderful sense to have and to hold through life. We had this sense when we were young. We could conger up the most outlandish things. We scared ourselves with ghoulish beings under the bed or fancies of wonderful happenings but as we grew older, we starting calling them dreams or wishes. But imaging is more than just wakeful dreams.

What is it to imagine? Why is it that some people are able to continue through life with the blessing and talent to keep imagining? How was this talent developed, were they born with it or was it nurtured and encouraged when they were young? Can it be revived when it is lost?

My generation grew up with the genius of Walt Disney and his entire wonderful make-believe characters filling our lives with laughter and awe and sometimes scary things. He lived a life of imagination and created wonders in his time that the world fell in love with. It is true that each generation has given the world these talents. Today there are books and fairy tales and movies of incredible work by those whose imagination show no limits. We are blessed to have them. But how did they occur, what is it in a person that perpetuates such genius?

Dog Stories

These quotes and sayings were collected from many sources over a long time and not all were identifiable as to the authors.

"He is your friend, your partner, your defender, your dog. You are his life, his love, his leader. He will be yours, faithful and true to the last beat of his heart. You owe it to him to be worthy of such devotion."

– Unknown

A dog's philosophy: As you walk along the road of life remember to stop and smell—everything.

– Garfield

Friendship isn't about whom you have known the longest- it is about who came and never left your side.

– Unknown

(From a picture of a man and dogs footprint walking in the sand). You may have many friends but your dog has only one.

I live here you don't. If you don't want dog hair on your clothes stay off the furniture. My parents like me a lot better than most people. To you I am just a dog. To my parents I am an adopted child, who is black, furry, has four legs, barks and likes birds.

Doctor to patient: Go home and let your dog lick your face. Dog saliva is the most effective antidepressant you can get without a prescription.

My therapist has four legs and a wagging tail.

In order to keep a true perspective of one's importance, everyone should have a dog that will worship him and a cat that will ignore him.

Dogs live to make us happy. It's up to us to learn that lesson. Once a dog loves you, he loves you always, no matter what you do, no matter what happens no matter how much time goes by.

How to handle stress like a dog: If you can't eat it or play with it then piss on it and walk away.

"I come home and my room is bigger when my dog is there to greet me.

– James Michener from his book, Chesapeake."

A new study shows that dogs are smarter than cats. The dog: "Really? Haven't we gotten beyond labels? How about we stop comparing and celebrate all creatures. The droll, friendly, loving, loyal heroic ones and the cold, aloof tuna breath ones."

– Millard Filmore

Just a Dog: Author Unknown

From time to time, people tell me, lighten up, "it's just a dog", or, "that's a lot of money for just a dog."

They don't understand the distance traveled, the time spent, or the costs involved for "just a dog." Some of my proudest moments have come about with "just a dog."

Many hours have passed and my only company was "just a dog," but I did not feel once slighted or alone. Some of my saddest moments have been brought about by" just a dog," and in those days of darkness, the gentle touch of "just a dog" gave me comfort and reason to overcome the day. If you, to think it's:" just a dog," then you will probably understand phrases like "just a friend," "just a sunrise," or "just a promise."

"Just a dog" brings into my life the very essence of friendship, trust, and pure unbridled joy. "Just a dog" brings out compassion and patience that make me a better person. Because of "just a dog" I will rise early, take long walks and look longingly into the future.

So, for me and folks like me, it's not "just a dog" but an embodiment of all the hopes and dreams of the future, the fond memories of the past, and the pure joy of the moment.

"Just a dog" brings out what's good in me and diverts my thoughts away from myself and the worries of the day. I hope that someday they can understand that it's not "just a dog" but the thing that gives me humility and keeps me from being "just a man."

So, the next time you hear the phrase "just a dog" just smile, because they just don't understand.

Beauty: Robert Byrum

"Anyone who keeps the ability to see beauty never grows old."

– Unknown Author

Life brings changes to us all but Momma Natures beauty is forever persistent. She changes the scenes but never the script. She paints a new sunrise and sunset for us every day with a palate of new colors, always the master. What's nice is that we don't have to search for it, it flows all around us, we only have to recognize and appreciate her efforts.

She shows us many things:

A colorful sunset sky at the end of the day casting the last glimpse of earth and sea as it slowly fades for its nights rest.

An Autumn moon gray and silver in radiance shining on a forest ground covered with snow, casting moonlight shadows.

An early morning hoarfrost coating the landscape with reflecting sparkles.

Noisy wild geese on a sunny dawn, happy with the new day circling and landing on a plowed field.

A summer storm over the mountains, dark clouds bellowing ever upward chased by a flash of bright fire burning them as they cry out with earsplitting complaint.

The smell of rain as it cleans and washes the air.

She fills us with beautiful songs; a babbling brook tumbling over a rocky streambed; the wind soulfully blowing in the night; the hoot of an owl;

wild birds warbling melody's; a howling surf crashing into shore.

So many treasures for our taking.

"The thankful heart opens our eyes to a multitude of blessings that continually surrounds us."
    – James E. Faust

"If you foolishly ignore beauty, you'll soon find yourself without it. Your life will be impoverished. But if you wisely invest in beauty, it will remain with you all the days of your life."
    – Frank Lloyd Wright

Quotes and Bits of Knowledge
The six most important words; "I admit I made a Mistake"; The five most important words;

"You did a good job"; the four most important words; "What is your opinion?"; the three most important words; "If you please"; the two most important words; "Thank you."; the one most important word; "We or Why."

The least important word "I".

"Ignorance is preferable to error; and he is less remote from the truth who believes nothing, then he believes what is wrong."
    – Thomas Jefferson

Critical assessment of date is essential task of an educated mind.

Always remember there are two types of people in this world. Those who come into a room and say, "Well, here I am!" and those who come in and say "Ah, and there you are!"
    – Frederick Collins

"The true art of memory is the art of attention. The things we forget were never thoroughly embedded in our memory in the first place. The lapse is not a lack of memory but of initial concentration."

– Samuel Johnson

"Luck, is believing you're lucky and working like hell to make it happen. Luck is what happens when preparation meets opportunity."

– Seneca, Roman Philosopher 100AD

"They say these are not the best of times. But they are the only times I've ever known, and I believe there is a time for meditation in the cathedrals of our mind. For we are always what our situations hand us. It's either sadness or euphoria."

– Billy Joel

"Life is a great adventure and the worst of all fears is the fear of living it."

– Theodore Roosevelt

"Wise people can always find a way to bring out a smile."

– Buda

"It's healthy and important to keep a good sense of humor. Laughter is like music; it lifts your spirits. You grow happier as you mature with greater patience and love for others. There is a change in perception, a broadening, that comes with age, a greater appreciation for simple things. But you have to love yourself first. I now have a heightened appreciation of everyday life and feel more deeply how precious our time on Earth is."

– Tina Turner, Entertainer

The true meaning of life is to plant a tree; under whose shade you do not expect to sit.

Eventually, the tech world of today will create more problems, more destruction, more pain and suffering for mankind than it has ever been beneficial. It has already started and will continue.

– Byrum

"Democracy destroys itself because it abuses its right to freedom and equality. Because it teaches its citizens to consider audacity as a right, lawlessness as a freedom, abrasive speech as equality and anarchy as progress."

– Isocrates, 436-338 BC (Does this sound familiar in today's happenings?)

Freedom of the Press: "Be not intimidated, therefore, by any terrors, from publishing with the utmost freedom whatever can be warranted by the laws of your country, nor suffer yourselves to be wheedled out of your liberty by any pretenses of politeness, delicacy, or decency. These as they are often used, are but three different names for hypocrisy, chicanery and cowardice."

– Advice to the press by John Adams, 1765

"Let reverence for the laws be breathed by every American mother to the lisping babe that prattles on her lap; let it be taught in schools, seminaries, and in colleges; let it be written in primers, spelling books, and almanacs; let it be preached from the pulpit, proclaimed in legislative halls, and enforced in courts of justice. And, in short, let it become the political religion of the nation."

– Abraham Lincoln

View the whole world and with impartial eyes,
Consider and examine all that rise;
Weigh well their actions, and their treacherous ends,
How greatness grows, and by what steps ascends;
What murders, treasons, perjuries, deceit,
How many fall, to make one monster great? Author Unknown

"Never refer to your wedding night as the "original amateur hour."

– Phyllis Diller

"Trust your husband, adore your husband, and get as much as you can in your own name."

– Joan rivers

Chase your own dream, don't follow someone else. Reading or thinking of stories is all right but living them is better.

> *My child,*
>
> *In the life ahead of you, keep your capacity for faith and belief, but let your judgment watch what you believe. Keep your love of life, but throw away your fear of death. Life must be loved or it is lost, but it should never be loved to well. Keep your wonder of great and noble things, like sunlight and thunder, the rain and the stars, and the greatness of heroes. Keep your heart hungry for new knowledge. Keep your hatred of a lie, and keep your power of indignation. I am ashamed to leave you an uncomfortable world, but someday it will be better. And when that day comes, you will thank God for the greatest blessing man can receive, living in peace.*

Letter from an executed Yugoslav partisan to his unborn child in World War II.

Hypocrisy—Woe unto them that call evil good, and good evil; that put darkness for light, and light for darkness; that put bitter for sweet, and sweet for bitter!

– Old Testament, Isaiah 5:20

Life isn't about waiting for the storm to pass. It's about learning to dance in the rain.

"While we talk, hateful time runs on. Size the fruits of today, never rely on the future."

– Horace, Roman Poet, 65BC

"We think sometimes that poverty is only being hungry, necked and homeless. The poverty of being unwanted, unloved and uncared for is the greatest poverty." Mother Teresa

"Never doubt that a small group of thoughtful committed citizens can change the world. Indeed, it is the only thing that ever has."
 – Margaret Mead

The Art of Losing a Poem by Elizabeth Bishop, 1927-1974

The art of losing isn't hard to master

So many things seem filled with the intent to be lost that their loss is no disaster

Lose something every day. Accept the fluster of lost door keys, the hour badly spent

The art of losing isn't hard to master

Then practice losing faster: places and names, and where it was you meant to travel

None of these will bring disaster

I lost my mother's watch and look! My last or next to last houses went

The art of losing isn't hard to master

I lost two cities, lovely ones. And vaster some realms I owned, two rivers, a continent, I miss them, but it wasn't a disaster

Even losing you (the joking voices a gesture I love) I shan't have lied. It's evident the art of losing not hard to master though it may look like a disaster.

Architecture is the art of organizing a mob of craftsman.
 – Oscar Wilde

Human beings are the only creatures on earth that claim there is a God and the only living thing that behaves as if it hasn't got one.

Tennyson: From the Poem "Ulysses"

How dull it is to pause, to make an end,
To rust un-burnished, not to shine in use
As though to breath were life!

"Because there is no cosmic point to the life that each of us perceives on this distant bit of dust at galaxy's edge, all the more reason for us to maintain in proper balance what we have here. Because there is nothing else, nothing. This is it. And quite enough, all in all."
– Gore Vidal (1926-2012) On no existence beyond this one.

"It's not what you look at, it's what you see. Most people never observe what they look at."
– Henry David Thoreau

"All our discontents about what we want appear to me to spring from the want of thankfulness for what we already have."
– From the book Robinson Crusoe, published in 1719

"Let food be thy medicine and medicine be thy food."
– Hippocrates, 2300 year ago

Quotes: What is required for a good life? Author Unknown

Every man dies, not every man lives

You reflect on your face what is passing through your mind

The world stands on deceit & life is an illusion

Live life as simple as sunrise and sunset

Travel is "life outside the everyday bubble".

Get out of your comfort zone.

"Don't evaluate your life in terms of achievements, trivial or monumental, along the way. If you do, you will be destined to frustration of always seeking out other destinations, and never allowing yourself actually to be fulfilled. Instead, wake up and appreciate everything you encounter along your path. Enjoy the flowers that are there for your pleasure. Tune in to the sunrise, the little children, the laughter, the rain and the birds. Drink it all in…. there is no way to happiness: happiness IS the way."

– Dr. Wayne W. Dyer

There is a new data base today for high school students to track who has "been making" out over the weekend. It's called "Hickeypedia."

– Comic strip "Zit", Scott Borgmon

Friendship: Robert Byrum

It is me or was it the generation I grew up in? It seems to me that today the development of real lasting friendships is fleeting. Could it be that because we keep in such close contact with all of our technical toys; cell phones, e-mail etc. that we fail or fall in the habit of neglecting the small meaningful actions that glue and hold together a lifetime of friendship?

Could it be the old axiom "familiarity breeds contempt" as opposed to "absents makes the heart grow fonder?" Are we losing the old art of conversation with our use of instant nonessential and nonsensical sound bites? Is the present generation to grow up in a world where they cannot sit down and converse intelligently face to face? What will happen as they grow older when the novelty of these times and their toys wear off as surely, they will?

"Excellence is not an act but a habit. We are what we repeatedly do."

– Aristotle

I have a Labrador like personality- I'm happiest when I have a job to do.

If you look closely, you will see that the wrinkles on the faces of the happiest men and women point upward.

By experience we find the short way be long wandering.

Be ambitious and patient for the bigger things. Only moderate aspirations are fulfilled quickly. The present dies unless it is multiplied for the future.

"The history of religion is that of a shivering frightened people who have attempted to put a roof over their heads against the night and the fears and terror of the unknown. That is why man invented God. How many Gods since the beginning of time have been invented by man? Thousands, perhaps millions of them, all with different names, shapes, natures and powers."
– Irving Stone

Any religion that through dictate, political pressure or collusion that controls the action of an individual or group of individuals against their wishes is tyranny. Religious powers should not be able to dictate what is good or bad for individuals or a nation.
– Byrum

Belief that something is true without evidence is a presumption. A belief that persists, despite evidence to the contrary is a myth. Understanding supported by good evidence is a fact.

"Labor of the hands, even when pursued to the verge of drudgery, is perhaps never the worst form of idleness. It has a constant and imperishable moral, and to the scholar it yields a classic result."
– Henry David Thoreau

"Build on resolve and not regret
The structure of the future.
Waste no tears upon the blotted record of lost years,
But turn the leaf and smile."
– Adlai E. Stevenson

About "Urgency." Live as if you were to die tomorrow. Learn as if you were to live forever."

– Gandhi

Worry: "If only the people who worry about their liabilities would think about the riches they do possess, they would stop worrying. Would you sell both your eyes for a million dollars, or your two legs, or your hands or your hearing? Add up what you have, and you will find that you won't sell them for all the gold in the world. The best things in life are yours, if you can appreciate yourself. That's the way to stop worrying and start living."

– Dale Carnegie

If you think you are too small to make a difference, try getting in bed with a mosquito.

Life does come with a restart button you just have to find where to look.

"Try again, fail again. Fail better."

– Beckett

"The devil has put a penalty on all things we enjoy in life. Either we suffer in health or we suffer in soul or we get fat."

– Albert Einstein

"In any moment of decision, the best thing you can do is the right thing, the next best thing is the wrong thing, and the worst thing you can do is nothing."

– Theodore Roosevelt.

"Do not neglect gratitude. Say thank you. Better still, say it in writing. A simple note of thanks is money in the bank and you will be remembered."

– Princess Jackson Smith

Do more than sip at life, gulp the cup.

Life may not be the party we hoped for, but while were here we might as well dance.

"Only two things are infinite, the universe and human stupidity, and I'm not sure about the former."
 – Albert Einstein

"Religions are all alike-founded on fables and mythologies."
 – Thomas Jefferson

"Happiness is not a station you arrive at, but a manner of traveling."
 – Margaret Lee Runbuck

If you would be happy for a week, take a wife; if you would be happy for a month, kill a pig; but if you be happy all your life, plant a garden.
 – Ancient Chinese proverb

"One of the nicest things about life is the way we must regularly stop whatever we are doing and devote our attention to eating."
 – Luciano Pavarotti

It is not how old you are but how you are old. And that is a choice.

Gastronomical perfection can be reached in these combinations: one person dining alone, usually on a couch or a hillside; two people, of no matter of what sex or age, dining in a good restaurant; six people, of no matter what sex or age, dining in a good home.

"You learn in life that the only person you can really change is yourself. Now we are taught you must blame your father, your sisters, your brothers, the school, the teacher; you can blame anyone, but never yourself. It's never your fault. But it's ALWAYS your fault, because if you wanted to change, you're the one who has got to change. It's as simple as that."

– Katharine Hepburn

Resolutions: From the credo of Al-Anon

Just for today I will not brood about yesterday or obsess about tomorrow. I will not set far reaching goals or try to overcome all of my problems at once. I know I can-do something for twenty -four hours that would overwhelm me if I had to keep it up for a lifetime. Just for today: I will be happy. I will not dwell on thoughts that depress me. If my mind fills with clouds, I will chase them away and fill it with sunshine.

Just for today I will improve my mind. I will read something that requires effort, thought and concentration. I will not be a mental loafer.

Just for today I will make a conscious effort to be agreeable. I will be kind and courteous to those who cross my path, and I will not speak ill of others. I will improve my appearance, speak softly and not interrupt when someone else is talking. Just for today, I will refrain from improving anyone but myself.

Just for today, I will do something to improve my health. If I am overweight, I will eat healthfully, if only just for today. Just for today: I will gather the courage to do what is right and take responsibility for my own actions.

Coffee is the performance drug for seniors. Where the only performance required constitutes getting out of bed in the morning.

Coffee is Mother Nature's jumper cables.

– Garfield

"All too will bear in mind this sacred principle, that the will of the majority is in all cases is to prevail, that will, to be rightful must be reasonable; that the minority possess their equal rights, which equal laws must protect, and to violate would be oppression." Thomas Jefferson first inaugural address, 1801.

"The first wealth is health," said Emerson. It's an old truth, but one which bears repeating. The man who wants to work and to live life to the fullest cannot take his health for granted. He must take care of himself. "He who has health has hope and he who has hope has everything" goes an old proverb. Guard your health as if it were your most precious possession. It is.

When plunder becomes a way of life for a group of men living in a society, they create for themselves, in the course of time, a legal system that authorizes it and a moral code that glorifies it.
    – Byrum

Never bet against the stupidity of the American citizen.
    – For confirmation read Dear Abby.

"Injustice anywhere is injustice everywhere."
    – Martin Luther King

"I believe humans get a lot done, not because we are smart but because we have thumbs so we can make coffee."
    – Flash Rosenburg

"What I learned constructive about woman is that no matter how old they get, always think of them the way they were on their best day."
    – Ernest Hemingway

The only problem with love at first sight is that most people are too cheap to buy glasses.

> "Nor let soft slumber close your eyes
> Before you've recollected trice
> The train of actions through the day:
> Where have my feet chose out the way?

What have I learnt where're I've been?
From all I've heard, from all I've seen?
What know I more that's worth the knowing?
What have I done that's worth the doing?
What have I sought that I should shun?
What duty have I let undone;
Or into what follies run?
These self-inquiries are the road
That leads us to virtue. "
   – Isaac Watts

"First, they ignore you, then they laugh at you, then they fight you and then you win."
   – Ghandi

"It's important to run not on the fast track, but on your own track. Pretend you have only six months to live. Make three lists: the things you have to do, want to do, and neither have to do nor want to do. Then, for the rest of your life, forget everything in the third category."
   – Robert S. Eliot

"You cannot step in the same river twice. Change is the only constant in life."
   – Heraclitus

Anyone who keep the ability to see beauty never grows old.

"Whatever befalls the earth befalls the sons of the earth."
   – Seattle (Indian Chief)

"To the house of a friend, if your pleased to retire,
You must all things admit, you must all things admire;
You must pay with observance the price of your treat,
You must eat what is praised, and must praise what you eat."
    – George Crabbe

"Just as solid rock is not shaken by the storm, even so the wise are not affected by praise or blame."
    – Buda

"Finish each day before you began the next and impose a solid wall of sleep between the two. What is a weed? A plant whose potential has not been discovered."
    – Ralph Waldo Emerson

"What to a slave is the 4th of July?"
    – Frederick Douglass

Two men were meeting in a bar when the subject of Green Bay, Wisconsin, came up. The first man said, "it's a real nice place." The second responded, "What's nice about it. Only things ever come out of Green Bay are the Packers and ugly whores.' Now wait a minute, you son of a-bitch," said the first man. "My wife is from Green Bay." "Oh," the other replied. "She is? What position does she play?" Now that's real tact and quick thinking!
    – Dr. Wayne Dyer

The true meaning of freedom is to wake up in the morning and decide what to do with the rest of the day and to be able to pee wherever and whenever you want.
    – Byrum

"When science discovers the center of the universe a lot of people will discover that they are not it."
    – Bernard Baily

The reductions of flows of the Gulf Stream due to the reduction of salinity by freshwater melt of the Greenland glaciers due to climate change is a perfect example of multiple effects of a single act. The thinning of the sea ice in the Arctic is another. How will both of these events affect the ecology of the immediate area and far-reaching areas?

– Byrum

"Great beauty, great strength and great riches are really and truly of no great value. A right heart exceeds all. If you would have a faithful servant, and one that you like, serve yourself."

– Ben Franklin

Life is never a question of accumulating material things but in widening and deepening the sensitivity of the facilities of an awareness of the world in which we live. Always take a cargo of memories with you for when all else is lost the memories will remain and let the days leave tracks upon your memories.

– Louis L'Amour

"Cultivate the habit of early rising. It is unwise to keep the head long on the level of the feet."

– Henry David Thoreau

Dedicated to the young and the significance of change in your world; why should you worry or care?

1. The oceans are not rising fast

2. The severe storms are not affecting me

3. Oh, so in 2100 the world will change due to climate change. So, what, that's a long time away.

4. You are 20, soon faster than you think you will be 70. What will your world be like then? Will you really try to understand what's happening now or will you live one party after another until the party is over and

the reality of what is or has been occurring hits you in the face. You live today in a wonderland of material toys; TV, I-Pads, Twitter and on and on. For how long? Realize they are just toys; new ones will come and today's trinkets will fade. Your world is warming at a rate not experienced in the last 10,000 years. At least realize what is happening and possibly dedicate yourself to do something about it.

– Byrum

"There are only two days of the year that nothing can be done. One is called yesterday and the other is called tomorrow. Today is the right day to love, believe, do, and mostly live."

– Dalai Lama

'The earth has music for those who listen."

– George Santayana

"Nature will flow into you as sunshine flows into trees."

– John Muir

"There are always flowers for those who want to see them."

– Henri Matisse

All bird songs are love songs.

You speak of God. I ask which God? The God of the Christians; the God of the Jews; the God of the Muslims; the Hindu God, Buda? Maybe you speak of all the hundreds of pagan Gods of the Greeks and Romans? Or is it the Gods of the ancient Egyptians? There has been thousands of Gods down the path of history and remember they were all created by man.

– Byrum

Never let an asshole rent space in your head. Don't suffer fools gladly.

"I hope we crush in its birth the aristocracy of our moneyed corporations which dare already to challenge our government to a trial of strength and bid defiance to the laws of our country."

– Thomas Jefferson

Mother Nature is the greatest terrorist of them all. Piss her off with global warming, over population, pollution, etc. and she will bite us back as severely as the greatest weapons of mass destruction. It has already started and she is getting mean.

– Byrum

Waking up is an annoying way to start the day.

"The only true wisdom is what you don't know."

– Socrates

There are two ways to be fooled. One is to believe what isn't true, the other is to refuse to believe what is true. Who is being fooled today in 2021?

"It's not the will to win that matters. It is the will to prepare to win that matters."

– Paul Bryant

"Ethel," Gershwin asked her during intermission, "do you know what you're doing?" "No," she said. "Well," he replied, "never go near a singing teacher."

– George Gershwin to Ethel Merman

"The dream is in the mind; the realization of the dream is in the hands. Success is more attitude than aptitude. It is important to listen with all the senses and to feel. Awareness is a way of learning. Let the days leave tracks on your memories."

– Louis L'Amour.

Age is what you decide what you want it to be.

What shapes us is not so much the possessions we acquire but the memories we accumulate.

Enemies are good for a man. It keeps him from getting careless with himself.

Hope is not a plan. Planning without action is futile; action without planning is fatal. People don't plan to fail they just fail to plan.

"It should be the function of medicine to have people die young as late as possible."
 – E. Wynder

"Let your maidservant be faithful and strong and homely."
 – Ben Franklin

"Forgiveness liberates the soul. That is why it is such a powerful weapon."
 – Nelson Mandela

"I am an old man and I have suffered many misfortunes most of which never happened."
 – Mark Twain

 Subjects for Frequent Reflection
I am sure to be old, I cannot avoid aging
I am sure to be sick I cannot avoid sickness
I am sure to die, I cannot avoid death
All things dear and beloved to me are subject to change and separation
I am the owner of my actions; I will become the heir to my actions

Age is mind over matter. If you don't mind it doesn't matter.

Everybody is going to die. But we act as if we never will. If you don't want to die don't be born. If we are doomed to die let us spend.

Our Future: By Sapattana Sut

A monk reflects on this very body from the soles of his feet and on up, from the crown of his head on down, surrounded by skin and full of various kinds of un-clean things.

In this body there are head hairs, body hairs, teeth, skin, flesh, tendons, bones, bone marrow, kidneys, heart, lungs, liver, spleen, intestines-feces, bile, phlegm, pus, blood, sweat fat, tears, and urine.

Or again if we were to see a corpse cast away in a channel ground, picked at by crows and vultures, and hawks, by dogs, hyenas and various other creatures a skeleton smeared with flesh and blood connected with tendons.

A skeleton without flesh or blood or tendons scattered in all directions- the bones whitened then later decomposed into powder.

And he applies this to his very body. This body too; such as its nature, such as its future, such is its unavoidable fate.

"Be not puffed up with knowledge, and not proud because you are wise."

– Socrates 399 BC

"The narrow intelligence flashing from the eyes of a clever rogue is nor wisdom. A fool can learn to say all things a wise man says, and to say them on the same occasions but this is not wisdom."

– John Keyes

A doubtful friend is worst then certain enemy. Let a man be one or the other, and then we know how to meet him.

– Aesop's moral

We think ourselves sick and we become sick. We think ourselves well and we become well. We think ourselves sad and we become sad. We think ourselves happy and we become happy. We live as we think.

– Byrum

"Knowledge is a slow flowing river sometimes it backs up laden with debris, sometimes it runs dry. Sometimes a torrent. To move is to die a little, leaving behind the memories of the years. No truth is ugly and no lie is beautiful."

– Irvine Stone

On going to a bar to meet first- rate men. "If you want to catch trout, don't fish in a herring barrel."

– Ann Landers

"You know how I end relationships? I don't say, "This isn't working out." Or, "I don't want to see you anymore." This is a tip to remember, girls. If I never want to see a man again, I just say, "You know I love you, I want to marry you and have you children." Sometimes they make skid marks."

– Rita Rudner

"You must keep busy. Continue working if you can, or develop an interest that you can pursue as though it were a livelihood. Too many people look on retirement as a permanent vacation. They find that the vacation ends in a few weeks or months, leaving an empty future. Activity is the only antidote. People don't wear out, they give up."

– B.F. Skinner

A man with a hearing aid has a tactical advantage in any argument.

"Whoever said that the human race was not ingenious? It can turn an obvious truth into a falsehood and then sell the illusion to a repressed society as though it was the holy writ."

– Irvine Stone (Remind you of anyone today in 2021?)

"Live in the sunshine, swim in the sea, drink the wild air."
– Ralph Waldo Emerson

"Always go to other people's funerals, otherwise they won't come to yours."
– Yogi Berra

We live on this lovely piece of the world. It is ours to enjoy now, but not forever. It is only borrowed, it's a good feeling that it will be enjoyed by others. We live in a house we designed and built that sets on the side of a timbered mountain in the precise direction we wanted it to face with large windows taking in the distant mountains, the sunrise and a lake. Beautiful sunsets every day casting shadows. It is indeed a happy place that we named Shadow Pines.
– Bob & Nancy Byrum

"All animals are equal but some animals are more equal than others."
– George Orwell, in Animal Farm comparing people.

"I wouldn't listen to the naysayers and haters. The people who succeed are the people who don't quit."
– C. Lanper

Never tell people what to think. Just beg them to think.

"When man ignite in their hearts a religious fury, they inflict at the same time blindness upon their eyes."
– James Michener

Justice isn't something you receive it is what you inflict and if are not willing to inflict it you will never receive it. We must stand on principal or we will not stand at all. We are becoming a society in which has contempt for the rule of law.
– Byrum

"The past is gone, the future is not here, and if we do not go back to ourselves in the present moment, we cannot be in touch with life."

– Thich Nath Hahn

"If I were asked to give what I consider the single most useful bit of advice for all humanity, it would be this: Expect trouble as an inevitable part of life, and when it comes, hold your head high, look it squarely in the eye and say, "I will be bigger than you. You cannot defeat me." Then repeat to yourself the most comforting of all words, "This too shall pass." Maintaining self- respect in the face of a devastating experience is of prime importance."

– Ann Landers

"Just don't give up trying what you really want to do. Where there's love and inspiration, I don't think you can go wrong."

– Ella Fitzgerald

Sometimes you feel like a bullfrog on a busy street with your hopper broken.

I used to think that the brain was the most important organ. Then I thought look who's telling me that.

Many who sail on the sea of matrimony wished they had missed the boat.

Only a true hunter knows the anguish of the kill, and the appreciation of the killed.

"There is nothing wrong with change if it in the right direction. To improve is to change so to be perfect is to change often."

– Winston Churchill

"Childhood must pass away, and then youth, as surely as age approaches. The true wisdom is to be always seasonable, and to change with a good grace in changing circumstances. To love playthings well as a child, to lead an adventurous and honorable youth, and to settle

when the time arrives, into a green and smiling age, is to be a good artist in life and deserve well of yourself and your neighbor."
　– Robert Louis Stevenson

"Progress is impossible without change and those who cannot change their minds cannot change anything."
　– George Bernard Shaw

"You never lose by loving. You always lose by holding back."
　– Barbara De Angles

There are individuals in this world today who have evolved from a broken branch of evolution.

Character consists on what you do on the third and fourth tries.

"When a man is drowned in a party (political party), plunged in it beyond his depth, he runneth a great hazard of being on ill terms with good sense of morality or both of them. Such a man can hardly be called a free agent, and for that reason he is very unfit to be trusted with the people's liberty after he hath given up his own."
　– British Lord Halifax, 300 years ago.

"The great enemy of clear language is insincerity."
　– George Orwell

"Always bear in mind that your own resolution to exceed is more important than any other."
　– Abraham Lincoln

"The probability that we may fail in the struggle ought not to deter us from the support of a cause we believe to be just."
　– Abraham Lincoln

"The best things are nearest, breath in your nostrils, light in your eyes, flowers at your feet, duties at your hand, the path of Right just before you. Do not grasp at the stars, but do life's plain common work as it comes, certain that daily duties and daily bread are the sweetest things."
– Robert Louis Stevenson

"When you take a flower in your hand and really look at it it's your world for a while."
– Georgia O'Keeffe

What is a friend? When is a friend a friend and not merely an acquaintance? Define for yourself the true meaning of a friend.
– Byrum

"Be careful to leave your sons well instructed rather than rich, for the hopes of the instructed are better than the wealth of the ignorant."
– Epictetus

Good times never come back. Recognize them now and enjoy them with all your efforts while you can.

"Shake off all the fears of servile prejudices, under which weak minds are servilely crouched. Fix reason firmly in her seat, and call on her tribunal for every fact, every opinion. Question with boldness even the existence of God, because if there is one, he must more approve of the homage of reason than that of blind faith."
– Thomas Jefferson

If you are going to fart don't tighten up, it stains the arse and remember a fart correctly deployed can be used as effective weaponized methane.

A law that fails to protect the humble disgraces the name it bears.

Sex: By "Ovid," a famous poet in the First Century BC, known for his scandalous verse.

Be advised by me, do not come too sone to the climate of your pleasure, but by skillful holding back, reach it gently, do not, by setting to much sail, leave your mistress behind you; nor let her get too much in front of you. Row together towards the port. Voluptuousness reaches its greatest height when, overcome by it, lover and mistress are overcome at the same time. This ought to be your rule when there is no hurry and you are not compelled by fear of discovery to hasten your furtive pleasure. But if there is any danger in your taking your time, then bent over the oars, row with all your strength, and press your spurs into the thighs of your steed.

Woman, let pleasure penetrate even to the marrow of your bones, and let the enjoyment be equally divided between you and your lover. Whisper tender words, murmur softly, and let licentious suggestions sharpen your sweet spot.

Do not let too strong a light come into your bedroom. There are in beauty a great many things which are enhanced by being seen only in a half-light.

Treat others as you would like to be treated. The road to self-interest usually ends in isolation. When we greet the world with kindness and expect kindness in return, we know we are not alone.

Ignorance is unfortunate. Willful ignorance is stupid.

The Virus of 2020

The dumb uninformed may have an excuse but the stupid informed have none. To ignore the country's medical experts continually and put their own and others' lives in danger is the highest form of stupid. How many of these individuals have died by their own hands?

   – Byrum

"Through reality shows and the internet we have been fed a steady stream of incivility that models rude behavior. We have become used

to people treating others badly, it doesn't shock us anymore. But the end of civility marks the end of life as we know it. Do we really aspire to be citizens of the world that doesn't value regard for one another?"
    – Oprah

People (and our animals) live as long as you love and remember them.

"What is life? It is the flash of a firefly in the night. It is a breath of a buffalo in the wintertime. It is the little shadow that runs across the grass and louses itself in the sunset."
    – Chief Crowfoot, Blackfoot Indian Chief

"We make a living by what we get We make a life by what we give."
    – Winston Churchill

"Life can be wildly tragic at times, and I've had my share. But whatever happens to you, you have to keep a slightly comic attitude. In the final analysis, you have got not to forget how to laugh."
    – Katharine Hepburn

"Frame your mind to mirth and merriment,
which bars a thousand harms and lengthens life.
    – Shakespeare's -The Taming of the Shrew

Our ability as a society to separate truth from lies is under unprecedented threat. The truth comes naturally but lying takes the effort of a smart and devious flexible mind.

"When you "assume" you make an "ass" out of yourself."
    – Uma Thurman

"Keep your eyes on the gold. It never fades in beauty. Woman? They fade and grow shapeless and crusty with age. But woman are forever young when you have the gold."
    – Mark Twain

"There are times when it is hard to believe in the future, when we are temporarily just not brave enough. When this happens concentrate on the present. Cultivate happiness until courage returns. Look forward to the beauty of the next moment, the next hour, the promise of a good meal, sleep, a book, a movie, the immediate likelihood that tonight the stars will shine and tomorrow the sun will rise. Sink roots into the present until the strength grows to think about tomorrow."
   – Ardis Whitman

"Each of us must do what we must. If the wolf must die that my sheep may live so, be it. But I need not hate the wolf for what is his nature."
   – Louis L'Amour

Common sense is a flower that doesn't grow in everyone's garden.

Seasickness: "At first you are so sick you wish you would die then you are so sick you are afraid you won't."
   – Mark Twain

Man may plan, they may dream and struggle but the buzzard has only to wait for all things come to him in the end.

That's life. You set your alarm for six o'clock and the worm sets his for five thirty.

"There are two things money can't buy, love and time. You can buy a lot of things with money but love and time are so important, and they become more precious as life goes along."
   – Warren Buffett

"Wit, makes its own welcome and levels all distractions."
   – Ralph Waldo Emerson

"Hell is truth seen too late. When you are going through hell keep going. Success is walking from failure to failure with no loss of enthusiasm."
 – Winston Churchill

"I have no desire to die rich. I would rather be related to people who do."
 – Martin Mull

Observe three beautiful women standing together or one beautiful woman standing alone; a group of beautiful trees standing together or a single beautiful tree standing alone; a single beautiful horse standing in lovely meadow or a group of houses. Look closely, beauty is always more impressive when it stands alone.
 – Byrum

"The earth laughs at flowers."
 – Ralph Waldo Emerson

"Procrastination is opportunities assassin."
 – Victor Kiam

Sitting still and wishing
Makes no person great.
The good Lord sends us fishing
But you have to dig the bait.
 – Anonymous

"There is no elevator to success, you have to take the stairs."
 – Zig Ziglar

"I have lived to know that the great secret of human happiness is this: Never suffer your energies to stagnate. The old adage of "too many irons in the fire," conveys an untruth, you cannot have too many interests and objectives."
– Adam Clark

"The man who pursues happiness wisely will aim at the possession of many subsidiary interests in addition to those central ones upon which his life is built."
– Bertrand Russell

"Cleave ever to the sunny side of doubt."
– Alford Lord Tennyson

"When you enemies are destroying themselves do not interfere."
– Napoleon Bonaparte

People are not to be considered books containing a single page. Each person contains many pages and many contain volumes of books.

If you can solve your problems then what's the need of worrying? If you cannot solve them what is the need of worrying?

"Whatever you may look like, marry a man your own age—as your beauty fades, so will his eyesight."
– Phyllis Diller

"In marriage do thou be wise, prefer the person before money; virtue before beauty; the mind before body."
– William Penn

"When you meet someone, who can cook and do housework, don't hesitate a minute—marry him."
– Joey Adams

A Way of Life, author unknown
"Be aware and happy with what you got. If you can't change it don't let it bother you. The first thing in the morning when you get up drink a big glass of water. Be active. If you don't use it, you lose it so be active. Look at the good things; get rid of the bad things. If there is someone who is constantly dragging you down, don't have anything to do with them anymore. Go with the people who are positive."

"Love labor: for if thou dost not want it for food, thou mayst for physic. It is wholesome for the body, and good for thy mind. It prevents the fruits of idleness which many times comes of nothing to do, and leads too many to do what is worse than nothing."
　– William Penn

You can always take one more step; if it's antagonizing or a painful step it's still going forward, one painful step, and another, and another. What happens when you take that one more step? You get there. Keep marching.
　– Byrum

"I went on a diet, swore off drinking and heavy eating for fourteen days. I lost two weeks."
　– Joe E Lewis

"Someone invented hugs to let people know you love them without saying anything."
　– Bill Kearse

On Maturity:
"Each age, like every individual, has its own characteristic intoxication; We must seek in each decade the joys natural to our years. If play is the effervescence of childhood, and love is the wine of youth, the solace of age is understanding. If you would be content in age, be wise and learn something every day. Education is not a task, it is long happiness, an ennobling intimacy with great men, an unhurried excursion into all

realms of loveliness and wisdom. If in youth we fell in love with beauty, in maturity we can make friends with genius."

– Will Durant

"The best way to get most husbands to do something is to suggest that perhaps their too old to do it."

– Shirley MacLaine

"Everyone is entitled to their own opinion but not their own facts."

– David Monahan

Three men came upon a female genie who promised to grant each a wish. The first man said I wish I were 25% smarter. The genie blinked and the man said I feel smarter already. The second man said I wish I were 50% smarter, again the genie blinked and the man said now I know things I never knew. The third man said I wish I were 100% smarter. The genie blinked and the man turned into a woman.

Four Life Lessons from a True Genius: By: Karla Peterson, Columnist, San Diego Union Tribune
You don't have to be an intellectual giant to appreciate Stephen Hawking. You just have to be human, Hawking died Wednesday March 7, 2018 in his home in England at the age of 76, and the fact that he lived so many decades longer than medical science said he would is one of the least amazing things about him. When he was diagnosed with a degenerative motor disease at the age of 21 Hawking was given just a few years to live. What we will remember most about him is not that he lived for 55 more years, but what he did with those 55 years and what we learned from them. When Hawking was given the miraculous gift of unexpected longevity, the world reaped the benefits. In memory of a single man here are some of the many life lessons we learned from Steven Hawking's rich years on our planet.

1.Don't Stop Believing

When the Oxford educated Hawking was first diagnosed with ALS (Lou Gehrig disease) in 1963, he fell into a deep and totally understandable depression. But he found new life in his relationship with fellow student Jane Wide, and despite dire prognosis, the couple got married and had three children together. Two years after his ALS diagnosis, Hawking received his doctorate from the university of Cambridge. He was elected to Britain's prestigious Royal Society at the age of 32, despite the fact that he was too frail to turn the pages of a book without help. After he was no longer able to talk, Hawking gave his speeches through a vocal synthesizer.

2. Don't Fence Yourself In

Hawking was almost completely paralyzed, but he visited every continent including Antarctica. He celebrated his 60th birthday in a hot air balloon, gave zero gravity flight a try five years later and hoped to travel to space via Richard Branson's Space ship Two. He even dared to play poker with Albert Einstein and Isaac Newton on an episode of "Star Track: The Next Generation." In each case, there was probably a chorus of level – headed voices telling Hawking that he had no business doing what he was thinking of doing, but he did it anyway. "I want to show that people need not be limited by physical handicaps as long as they are not disabled in spirit" Hawking said. Lesson learned professor H!

3. Make them Laugh

What can you say about a theoretical physicist who joked about his IQ on The Simpsons? One of four times he showed on the show, made a cameo appearance in the episode of "The Big Bang Theory" that was named after him. You can say that Hawking was smart enough to know that laughter is the life preserving gift that never stops giving. Over the years he reeled off quips about sex, morality and Homer Simpsons Doughnut Shaped Universe Theory. But when he talked about the importance of humor, he wasn't kidding. "Life would be tragic" he said "if it wasn't funny."

4. Life is an Imperfect Miracle, Cherish It

Even as a kid, Hawking was curious as to how things worked and why. He studied physics and astronomy because he was addicted to wonder, and he stayed that way. Hawking carried that sense of possibility with him as he made his journey into the center of our universe. And of all the nuggets of wisdom he scattered along the way this one is as a good parting gift as any.

"Remember to look up at the stars and not down at your feet Try to make sense of what you see and wonder what makes the universe exist. Be curious. And however difficult life may seem, there is always something you can do and succeed at."

– Stephen Hawking.

(His ashes were interned between two other great men in London at Westminster Abby: Isaac Newton, father of gravity and Charles Darwin, father of evolution.)

"The words a man speaks today live on in his thoughts or his memories of others, and the shot fired, the blow strut, the thing done is like a stone tossed in a pool, and the ripples keep widening out until they touch the lives far from ours."

– Louis L'Amour

Many men wish but never will. Every dream has a price that two few are willing to pay.

"Trust your happiness and the richness of your life at this very moment."

– Kathryn Ann Porter

To a fool time brings only age, not wisdom. The only real asset we have is time. Without time nothing else is possible. Be always short of time in your life but never in the things you use it for.

It isn't a sin to be wrong but it is a sin to know in your heart you are wrong and not admit it to yourself.
   – Byrum

"Autonomy and dominion over one's own body go to the very heart of what it means to be free."
   – In an opinion of the Iowa Supreme Court striking down abortion restrictions.

"Boastful men are the scorn of wise men, the admiration of fools, the idols of parasites and the slaves of their own vaunts."
   – Francis Bacon, 16th Century, and oh how true that is in 2021.

"Money is like manure, no good unless spread."
   – Francis Bacon

"Any refusal to recognize reality for any reason, has disastrous consequences. There is no evil thought except one, the refusal to think. The worst guilt is to accept an underserved guilt. Learn to value yourself, which means: to fight for your happiness."
   – Ayn Rand

"To remain alive, we must think. But to think is an act of choice. Reason does not work automatically; thinking is not a mechanical process; the connections of logic are not made by instinct. The function of your stomach, lungs and heart are automatic; the function of your mind is not. In any hour and issue of your life you are free to think or evade that effort. But you are free to escape from your nature, from the fact that reason is your means of survival-so for you that are a human being, the question "to be or not to be" is like the question "to think or not to think"."
   – Ayn Rand

"Believe in something even if it means sacrificing everything." Just do it.
 – Colin Kaepernick the professional quarterback who was the first to kneel.

There is a reason that today's book "Profile in Courage" is a thin volume. There is not a lot of it around anymore.
 – Tribute to John McCain.

"Truth is the foundation of Democracy."
 – Bob Woodward, author and investigative reporter.

> There is a long trail a winding
> Into the land of my dreams
> Where the nightingale is singing
> And the white moon beams
>
> There is a long, long night of waiting
> Until my dreams all come true
> Till the day I'll be going down
> That long, long trail with you

"Say "I love you" to those you love. The eternal silence is long enough to be silenced in, and that awaits us all."
 – George Eliot

Perseverance is stubbornness with a purpose. Hope is an unrelenting temptress.

They should make an alarm clock that sounds like a dog vomiting. Nothing makes me jump out of bed quicker.

"Commit yourself to a dream. Nobody who tries to do something great but fails is a total failure. Why/ Because he can always rest assured that he succeeded in life's most important battle- he defeated the fear of trying."

– Robert H. Schuller

"Always remember the distinction between contribution and commitment. Take the matter of bacon and eggs. The chicken makes a contribution. The pig makes a commitment."

– Herbert Spencer

"Twelve things to remember. 1. The value of time. 2. The success of perseverance. 3. The pleasure of working. 4. The dignity of simplicity. 5.The worth of character. 6. The power of kindness. 7. The influence of example. 8. The obligation of duty. 9. The wisdom of economy. 10. The virtue of patience. 11. The improvement of talent. 12. The joy of origination."

– Marshall Field.

To live? What is that? A mouse lives, a fly lives: one flees in terror, another lives in filth. They exist, they are alive, but do they live? To challenge the fates that is living. To ride the storms, to live nobly, not wasting one's life with too much wine.

– Unknown

Autumn is the second spring where every leaf is a flower. Love enters through the eyes.

"Study nature, love nature, stay close to nature, it will never fail you."

– Frank Lloyd Wright

"Optimisms important because it is a form of seeing what is possible and then helps make it a reality."

– Melinda Gates

"Sigh no more, ladies, sigh no more,
Men were deceivers ever,
One foot in sea, and one on shore,
To one thing constant never.
Then sigh not so, but let them go,
And be your blithe and bonny,
Converting all your sounds of woe
Into Hey nonny, nonny."
Shakespeare's Much Ado About Nothing

"Ask others about themselves and where are they from, at the same time be on guard not to talk too much about yourself."
– Mortimer Alder

On marriage: "Before you run in double harness, look carefully at the other horse."
– Ovid

"Do not think about trying to make it through a lifetime with a man. Just consecrate on making it through a year The reason a man will not try to split up with you after a year or so is his limitless fear of breaking in a new model."
– Stephanie Brush

Don't dig your grave with your knife and fork. English proverb

"A time comes to everyone when a choice has to be made, where a direction has to be taken."
– Samuel Adams, 1764

"The function of a free press is to provoke, not pacify."
– Horace Greely

"What we obtain too cheap we esteem lightly; it is dearness only that gives everything value."

– Thomas Paine

"What is the chief end of man? To get rich-in what way, dishonesty if we can; honest if we must. Who is God, the only and the true? Money is God, gold and greenbacks and stock- father son and the ghost of same- three persons in one, these are the true and only God, mighty and supreme." "The revised Catechism"

– Mark Twain

"The word God is for me nothing but the expression of and the product of human weakness, the Bible a collection of venerable but still rather primitive legends, no interpretations, no matter how subtle, can for me change anything about this."

– Albert Einstein

New year's resolution. A promise whose intentions outlast its action by about 364 days.

The Road Not Traveled- Robert Frost
I shall be telling this with a sigh

Sometimes ages and ages hence

Two roads diverged in a wood and I

And I took the one less traveled by

And that has made all the difference

Are we humans the "frog in the pan," do we lack the capacity to feel the water slowly boiling (climate change) and take action and jump or are we destined to boil slowly away in our own caldron? Are we crocking "economic growth, economic growth" until we boil? As we rightly increase wind and solar power, do we decrease the overall benefit by promoting growth for growth's sake? When will we attack all emissions? Until we do it's a zero-sum game and the world will lose.

– Byrum

Life of great men all remind us
We can make our lives sublime
And departing leave behind us
Footprints in the sands of time
    – Henry Wadsworth Longfellow

"If you need to buy things to store things perhaps you have too many things."
    – Gretchen Ruben

"Some folks will spare no amount of energy just to stay in a bad mood. Sedentary people are apt to have sluggish minds. A sluggish mind is apt to be reflected in flabbiness of body and in a dullness of expression that invites no interest and gets none."
    – Rose Fitzgerald Kennedy

"In question of power let no more be heard of confidence in man, but bind him down from mischief by the chains of the Constitution."
    – Thomas Jefferson

"All men who have power ought to be distrusted to a certain degree."
    – James Madison

"You can always count on Americans to the right thing after they have exhausted all other possibilities."
    – Winston Churchill

"Mark how fleeting and paltry is the estate of man, yesterday an embryo, tomorrow a mummy or ashes. So, for the hair's breath of time assigned to thee live rationally, and part with life cheerfully, as drops the ripe olive, extolling the season that bore it and the tree that matured it."

– Marcus Aurelius

"The King is not the law; the law is the King."

– Thomas Payne

The best thing you can do is quit while you're behind. You can only dig your hole (lies) so deep before it caves in on you.

– Byrum

It is easier to deceive a multitude then just one man. Oh, how true today in 2021.

Why when the foundation of education was being formed in the 5th century BC the teaching of ethics for young men in Greece was so important (starting at age 6), ethics is not taught to today's youth? In today's modern world it is certainly apparent that we need it. In the 5th and 6th Century's BC the teaching of moral values was deemed to be of great value. Why not today? Simple philosophy and moral values are needed.

– Byrum

When I want your advice, I'll give it to you.

"The only true measure of success is the ratio between what we might have done and what we might have been on the one hand, and the things we have made of ourselves on the other."

– HG Wells, English author, 1866-1946

Food that is "flavored with hunger" is the best food you have ever eaten.

The disappointment with Democracy is clear, it is present oriented. It has a hard time accepting pain today for gain tomorrow; it prefers what is popular to what is necessary and difficult.

"You must live in the present, you must launch yourself on every wave, find your eternity in each moment. Fools stand on their island of opportunities and look towards another land. There is no other land: there is no other life but this."
   – Henry David Thoreau

Emile Henry Gauvreau on Conformity – "I was part of that strange race of people described as spending their whole lives doing things, they detest to make money they don't want to buy things they don't need to impress people they dislike."

And now among the fading embers, these in the main are my regrets: When I am right no one remembers, when I am wrong no one forgets.

When I get up in the morning, I never let the "Old Man" into my day.

"We think sometimes that poverty is only being hungry, necked and homeless. The poverty of being unwanted, unloved and uncared for is the greatest poverty."
   – Mother Teresa

"No misfortune is so bad that whining about it won't make it worse."
   – Jeffery Holland

Gratitude turns what we have into enough. Alsop Saying.

"Do not shorten the morning by getting up late; Look upon it as the essence of life, as to a certain extent sacred."
  – Author Schppenhauer

"Green may be the turf above thee
Friend of my better days
None knew thee but to love thee
Nor name thee but to praise."
  – Halleck

"A well written life is almost as rare as a well-spent one. In every man's writing the character of the writer must be recorded."
  – Thomas Carlyle

"Ordinarily he is crazy; but he has lucid moments when he is only stupid."
  – Thomas Bayley

"The invasion of an army can be resisted, but not an idea whose time has come."
  – Victor Hugo

Ralph Waldo Emerson 1803-1882

  "Some of the hurts you have cured
  And the sharpest you have still survived
  But what torments of grief you endured
  From evils which have never arrived?"

"A friend is a person with whom I may be sincere, before him I may think aloud. The only reward of virtue is virtue; the only way to have a friend is to be one. Make yourself necessary to somebody. The only true gift is a portion of thyself. What astonishes men so much is common sense and plain dealing. Shallow men believe in luck. Nothing great was ever achieved without enthusiasm. Life is not so short that there is always time enough for courtesy. The true test of civilization is not census, not the size of cities; nor crops-no, but the kind of men the country turns out."

– Emerson

Abraham Lincoln 1809-1865

"If destruction is our lot, we must ourselves be its author and finisher. As a nation of free men, we must live through all times or die by suicide. There is no grievance that is a fit object of redress by mob law."

William Channing 1810-1884

"To live content with small means; to seek elegance rather than fashion; to be worthy, not respectable and wealthy, not rich; to study hard, think gently, act friendly; to listen to stars and birds, to babies and sages with open heart; to bear all cheerfully, do all bravely, await occasions, hurry never. This is to be my symphony."

William Thackery 1811-1863

"Remember, it's as easy to marry a rich woman as a poor one. Tis strange what a man may do to a woman yet think him an angle."

Henry David Thoreau 1817-1862

"Some circumstantial evidence is very strong, as when you find a trout in the milk. There are thousands hacking at the branches of evil to one striking at the root. A man is rich in proportion to the number of things which he can afford to let alone. Our life is frittered away by detail-Simplify, Simplify. Rather than love, then money give me truth. We need the tonic of wilderness- we can never have enough of nature.

Live in each season as it passes; breath the air, drink the drink, taste the fruit, and resign yourself to the influences of each."

Charles Kinsley 1819-1875

"When the world is young lad

And the trees are green

And every goose a swan lad

And every lass a queen

Then hay for the boat and horse lad

 And room the world away

Young blood must have a course lad

And every dog his day."

George Meredith 1828-1909

"I expect woman will be the last thing civilized by man. Kissing don't last; cooking does."

Charles Dudley Warner 1829-1900

"To own a bit of ground, to scratch it with a hoe, to plant seeds, and watch the renewal of life, this is the happiest delight of the race, the most satisfactory thing a man can do. What man needs in gardening is cast iron back with a hinge in it. A garden is a lovesome thing."

Edward Layton

"We may live without poetry, music and art. We may live without conscience, and live without heart. We may live without friends; we may live without books; but civilized man cannot live without cooks."

James Whistler 1834-1903

"I am not arguing with you. I'm telling you."

Mark Twain 1835-1910

"There are several good protections against temptations, but the surest is cowardice. Familiarity breeds contempt-and children."

Friedrich Nietzsche 1844- 1900

"Is not life a hundred times short for us to bore ourselves? Two great European narcotics, alcohol and Christianity. I call Christianity the one great curse, the one great instinct of revenge, for which no means are too venomous, to underhanded, to underground and petty- I call it the one immortal blemish of mankind."

Clarence Darrow 1857-1938

"I don't consider it an insult, but rather a compliment to be called an agnostic. I do not pretend to know what many ignorant men are sure of-that is all agnostic means."

Theodore Roosevelt 1858-1919

"I wish to preach not the doctrine of ignoble ease, but the doctrine of the strenuous life. No man is above the law and no man is below it, nor do we ask any man's permission when we require him to obey it. Obedience to the law is demanded as a right; not asked as a favor.

To waste, to destroy our natural resources, to skim and exhaust the land instead of using it so to increase its usefulness, will result in undermining in the days of our children the very prosperity which we ought by right to hand down to them."

Henry Mencken 1880-1956

"No one ever went broke underestimating the intelligence or taste of the American people."

Pearl S. Buck 1892-1973

"I feel no need for any other faith then my faith in human beings. I am so absorbed in the wonders of earth and life upon it that I cannot think of heaven and angles. I have enough for this life. If there is no other life, then this one has been enough to make it worth being born a human being."

Grouch Marx 1895-1977

"I never forget a face, but in your case, I'll make an exception."

Kahil Gibran 1883-1931

"You give but little when you give of your possessions. It is when you give of yourself that you truly give."

Adolf Hitler 1889-1945

"The greatest mass of the people more easily falls victims of a big lie then a small one." How true that is today in 2021!

Ogden Nash 1902-1971

"The turtle lives twist plated decks

Which practically conceal its sex

I think it cleaver of the turtle

In such a fix to be so fertile"

"There is only one way to achieve happiness on this terrestrial ball. And that is to have a clean conscience or none at all."

"Ten years ago, she split the air

To see what she could see

Tonight, she bumps against a chair,

Betrayed by milky eye.

She seems to pant, times up, times up

My little dog must die." Nash

"When I remember bygone days
I think how evening follow morn
So many I loved were not yet dead
So many I love were not yet born
How confusing the beams from memory's lamp are;
One day a bachelor, the next a grandpa.
What is the secret of this trick?
How did I get so old so quick?"
   – Nash

James Madison
"The accumulation of all powers, legislative, executive and judiciary in the same hands, whether of one, a few or many, whether hereditary, self-appointed or elected, may justly be pronounced the very definition of tyranny."

Dolly Parton
"I can't stop long enough to grow old. I'm just going to be the best that can I at whatever age I am. We just can't hope for a brighter day we have to work for a brighter day."

From the comic page "Pearls Before Swine", by Stephan Pastis
"Imagine there is no Facebook
It's easy if you try
No trolls to berate us
 Around us no more lies
Imagine all the crack 'pots
Silenced for the day
Imagine there's no Twitter
It isn't hard to do

Nothing to shill or cry for
And no re-tweeters too
Imagine all the people being kind to you
You may say I hate screamers
But I'm not the only one
Who hopes one day we will stop this
And the world will be more fun."

If luck happens when preparation meets opportunity what happens when laziness meets stupidity?
– Byrum

An oriental philosopher gave us this bit of wisdom: "The Sages do not consider that making no mistakes is a blessing. They believe, rather, that the great value of man lies in his ability to correct his mistakes and continually make a new man of himself."

Edison said he expected to live to 130 years. Asked how, he explained the figure was relative to his working hours to the average man's. "Overtime" accounts for most success.

"We cannot command nature except by obeying her."
– Francis Bacon

To Dare: Taking a Risk: Unknown author

To laugh is to risk appearing the fool. To weep is to risk appearing sentimental. To reach for another is to risk involvement. To expose your ideas, your dreams, before a crowd is to risk their loss. To love is to risk not being loved in return. To live is to risk dying. To believe is to risk failure. But risks must be taken, because the greatest hazard is to risk nothing. The people who risk nothing, do nothing, have nothing, and are nothing. They may avoid suffering and sorrow, but they cannot learn, feel, change, grow, love, live. Chained by their attitudes, they are slaves, they have forfeited their freedom. Only a person who risks is free.

"Take risks, be willing to put your mind and your spirit, your time and your energy, your stomach and your emotions on the line. To search for a safe place, to search for an end to a rainbow, is to search for a place that you will hate once you find it. The soul must be nourished along with the bank account and the resume. The best nourishment for any soul is to create your own risk."

– Jim Lehrer

"There is only one success, to be able to spend your life in your own way."

– C. Morley

"Sometimes, when you're feeling important, sometimes when your ego is in bloom, sometimes when you take it for granted, that you're the outstanding person in the room.

Sometimes when your feel you're going would leave an un-fill able hole- just follow these simple instructions in the interest of peace in your soul. Take a bucket and fill it with water, put your hand in it up to your wrist, pull it out and the hole that's remaining is a measure of how you will be missed. You may splash all you please when you enter, you can stir up the water galore, but stop and you'll find in a minute it looks quite the same as before.

There's a moral to this quaint example, do the best as you possibly can, be proud of yourself, but remember there is no indispensable man."

– Author Unknown

Youth: Author Unknown

"Youth is not a time of life; it is state of mind. It is not a matter of rosy cheeks, red lips and supple knees; it is a matter of the will, a quality of the imagination, vigor of the emotions; it is a freshness of the deep springs of life.

Youth means a predominance of courage over timidity, of adventure over the love of ease. This often exist in a man of sixty more than a boy of twenty. Nobody grows old merely by a number of years. We grow old by deserting our ideas.

Years may wrinkle the skin, but to give up enthusiasm wrinkles the soul. Worry, doubt, self-interest, fear and despair-these bow the heart and turn the sprit to dust.

Whether sixty or sixteen, there is in every human being's heart the love of wonder, the sweet amazement at the stars and star like things, the undaunted challenge of events, the unfailing childlike appetite for what's-next, and the joy of the game of living.

You are as young as your faith, as old as your doubt; as young as your self- confidence, as old as your fear; as young as your hope, as old as your despair."

Old Age: "Keep working as long as you can. Remember, you can't help getting older, but you don't have to get old. There is an old saying, "Life begins at 40." That's silly, life begins every morning when you wake up. Open you mind to it; don't just sit there, do things."

    – George Burns

"I don't believe in pessimism. If something doesn't come up the way you want, forge ahead. If you think it's going to rain, it will."

    – Clint Eastwood

Getting started is often the hardest part of the job. A person needs all his energy just for the starting. We're like cars, only a small percentage of engine power is necessary to run the car, but all its power may be necessary to start it.

The national Poetry contest had come down to two semifinalists. A Yale graduate and a redneck from Montana. They were given a word, and then allowed two minutes to study the word and come up with a poem that contained the word. The word was "Timbuktu".

The Yale man went first and said: "Slowly across the desert sand trekked a lonely caravan. Men on camels, two by two destination – Timbuktu."

The crowd went crazy. No way could the redneck top that.

The redneck calmly made his way to the microphone and recited: "Me and Tim hunting we went, met three whores in a pop-up tent. They were three and we were two, so I bucked one and Timbuktu two".

The redneck won hands down.
   – Author Unknown

Some people set low expectations for themselves and they achieve it with great effort.

"Success is walking from failure to failure with no loss of enthusiasm."
   – Winston Churchill

Patience: "The most extraordinary thing about the oyster is this. Irritations get into his shell. He does not like them. But when he cannot get rid of them, he uses the irritation to do the loveliest thing an oyster ever has a chance to do. If there are irritations in our lives today, there is only one prescription: make a pearl. It may have to be a pearl of patience, but, anyhow, make a pearl. It takes faith and love to do so."
   – Harry Emerson Fosdick

Bumpy roads lead to beautiful places.

"Life is not easy for any of us. But what of that? We must have perseverance and above all confidence in ourselves. We must believe we are gifted for something and this thing, at whatever cost, must be attained."

– Marie Curie

All the conflicts in the world, wars, political upheavals, immigration are secondary concerns. Climate change, now and in the future is the #1 concern that will make all other conflicts minor. Even today's virus.

– Byrum

"Every time you pass on a blind curve, every time you speed up on a slippery road, every time you step on it harder than your reflexes will safely take, every time you drive with your reactions slowed down by a drink or two, every time you follow the car ahead too closely, you're gambling a few seconds against blood and agony and sudden death."

– J. C. Furnas

Courage doesn't always roar, sometimes courage is the quite voice at the end of the day that says, I will try again tomorrow.

"Moral courage is a rarer commodity then bravery in battle."

– Robert Kennedy

"You only live once, but if you do it right once is enough."

– May West

Perseverance is stubbornness with a purpose. Persistence leads to luck.

"Love is the most durable power in the world."

– Martin Luther King

"If people would concentrate on the really importance things in life there would be a shortage of fishing poles."

– Doug Larson

"Life is short" really means "Do something."

– Ngozi Adichie

"Use your health even to the point of wearing it out. That is what it is for. Spend all you have before you die; do not out live yourself."

– Irish playwright George Bernard Shaw

"Nature will bear the closet inspection. She invites us to lay our eyes level with her smallest leaf and take an insect view of its plain."

– Henry David Thoreau

"When you lead with your nice foot forward, you win every time. It may not be today, it may not be tomorrow, but it comes back to you when you need it. We live in the age of instant gratification, of immediate likes, and it is uncomfortable to wait to see the dividends of your kindness. But I promise you it will appear exactly when you need it."

– Kristen Bell

Fresh air impoverishes the doctor.

– Danish Proverb

"The art of medicine consists of amusing the patient while nature cures the disease."

– Voltaire 1694-1778

"Don't gamble; take all of your savings and buy some good stock and hold it until it goes up. If it doesn't go up don't buy it."

– Will Rogers

"In general, the proof of a person's knowledge or intelligence is his ability to teach."

– Aristotle

"Nature's music gives us some of the best songs we can hear."

– Octavia Spencer

"Ever remain aware of your enemy's activities, secret or otherwise; never feel secure against his treachery against you and consider ways in which you might outwit him or defeat him."

– Prince of Gurgan 1082 AD

"Time is the coin of your life. It's the only coin you have and only you can decide how to spend it. Be careful, less other people spend it for you."

– Carl Sandburg

"Do not be dismayed by the brokenness of the world, all things break and all things can be mended. Not with time as they say, but with intention. So, go. Love intentionally, extravagantly, unconditionally. The broken world waits in darkness for the light which is you."

– L. R. Knost

Winston Churchill's favorite story: A man received a telegram about the death of his mother-in law and asked for instructions. He answered; "Embalm, Cremate, Bury at Sea, Take no chances."

"Do not make yourself miserable by thinking what may never happen. Is not today enough that you must think of tomorrow and the day after that? Yesterday is gone, you have today; tomorrow may never come. Do not cross bridges before you come to them nor clutter your mind with odds and ends that interfere with clear thinking."

– Author Unknown

Love is the food of marriage; let not yours starve.

An Irish Proverb: "The beginning of a ship is a board; of a kiln, a stone and the beginning of health is sleep."

It seems that man has always needed Gods, but did not the Gods also need man to create them?

Have we become immune to the virus? Are we slowly accepting as normal the daily increase and more tragic deaths? Are we treating these tragic events as road kill that we drive over and accept it as a normal part of our lives? We have lost 700,00 lives in less than a year. We will soon surpass the total number of Americans killed in four years during World War Two. Where is the nation's shock and anger that this is happening?

– Byrum

"Dost, thou love life. Then do not squander time; for that's the stuff life is made of."

– Benjamin Franklin

"Time is but a stream I go fishing in. I drink at it but while I drink, I see the sandy bottom and detect how shallow it is. Its thin current slides away but eternity remains."

– Henry David Thoreau.

George Washington's Farewell Address: "The alternate domination of one factor over another shaped by the spirit of revenge is itself a frightful despotism, sooner or later the chief of some prevailing fraction, more able or more fortunate than his competitors turn this deposit to the purpose of his own elevation on the ruins of public liberty." Today in 2021?

"The ignorance of just one voter in a Democracy, impairs the security of all."

– John F. Kennedy

Love is giving away the last piece of pizza you wanted.

People will not remember what you say but they will remember how you make them feel.

The woods would be very silent if no birds sang except those who sound the best.

"A properly functioning Democracy depends on an informed electorate. If a nation expects to be ignorant and free, in a state of civilization, it expects what never was and never will be. If we are to guard against ignorance and remain free it is the responsibility of every American to be informed."

– Thomas Jefferson

The Price They Paid: Author unknown

Have you ever wondered what happened to those men who signed the Declaration of Independence?

Five signers were captured by the British as traitors and tortured before they died. Twelve had their homes ransacked and burned. Two lost their sons in the Revolutionary Army, and another had two sons captured. Nine of the 56 signers fought and died from wounds or hardships of the Revolutionary War.

What kind of men were they? Twenty -four were lawyers and jurist. Eleven were merchants, nine were farmers and large plantation owners, men of means, well educated. But they signed the Declaration of Independence knowing full well that the penalty would be death if they were captured.

They signed and pledged their lives, their fortunes and their sacred honor.

Carter Braxton of Virginia, a wealthy planter and trader, saw his ships swept from the seas by the British navy. He sold his home and properties to pay his debts and died in rags.

Thomas McLean was so hounded by the British that he was forced to move his family almost constantly. He served in Congress without pay and his family was kept in hiding. His possessions were taken from him and poverty was his reward.

Vandals or soldiers or both looted the properties of Ellery, Clymer, Hall, Walton, Gwinnet, Heyward, Rutledge and Middleton.

John Hart was driven from his wife's bedside as she was dying. Their thirteen children fled for their lives. His fields and grist mill were laid waste. For more than a year he lived in forest and caves, returning home after the war to find his wife dead., his children vanished. A few weeks later he died from exhaustion and a broken heart.

Francis Lewis had his home destroyed. The enemy jailed his wife and she died within a few months.

At the battle of Yorktown, Thomas Nelson Jr. noted that the British general Cornwallis had taken over the Nelson home for his headquarters. The owner quickly urged General Washington to open fire, which was done. The home was destroyed and Nelson died bankrupt.

Such were the stories of the American Revolution. These were not wild-eyed rabble-rousing ruffians. They were soft-spoken men of means and education. They had security, but they valued liberty more. Standing straight, and unwavering they pledged: "For support of this declaration, with a firm reliance on the protection of the Divine Providence, we mutually pledge to each other, our lives, our fortunes and our sacred honor."

They gave us an independent America. Can we keep it? Where is this kind of dedication to our country now in 2021?

Where Do You Stand? By William G. Saltonstall, Principal of the Phillips Exeter Academy

One of our human failings as I see it, has been our admiration for the "Middle of the Roader." Certainly, many of us agree that the exercise of restraint is one of the marks of a good man. But in some areas compromise is flabby and dangerous. Any person of real conviction and strength must choose one side of the road or the other. It would be a strange kind of education that urged us to be "relative" honest, "sometimes" just, "usually" tolerant, "for the most part" decent.

As you read history and biography, I think you will not come to equate greatness with compromise. Rather, you will find it in decisiveness, combined with charity, gentleness and justice. There will be some wrong decisions, of course, but as long as mistakes are recognized the losses are far less serious than that occasioned by playing the middle of the road, sitting on the fence, undecided, unconvinced, incapable of strong feelings.

Life should be a continuous search for those people, those ideas and those causes to which we can gladly wholly give ourselves.

"Begin, be bold and venture to be wise"

– Horace

Lessons from a Dog; Author Unknown

"Never pass up the opportunity to go for a joy ride

Allow the experience of fresh air and wind in your face to be pure ecstasy.

When love one's come, always run to great them

When it's in your best interest, practice obedience

Let others know when they have invaded your territory

Take naps and stretch before rising

Run, romp and play daily

Eat with gusto and enthusiasm

Be loyal

Never pretend to be something you're not

If what you want lies buried, dig for it

When someone is having a bad day, be silent, set close and nuzzle them gently

Thrive on attention and let other people hug you

Avoid biting when a simple growl will do

When happy dance around and wag your whole body

No matter how often you're scolded or slighted, don't butt into the guilt thing and pout, run back and make friends

Delight in the simple joy of a long walk."

Climate Change: Robert Byrum

Global warming is a slow insidious disease causing the degrading of our planet on many fronts, a thousand pin prick to the heart of our precious earth. Slowly, it eats at the very core gradually destroying constantly but goes undetected or ignored by many. It is the warming of the seas, the killing of our forest, Amazon fires, the world-wide melting of the glaciers, the loss of the Arctic Sea ice, melting of Greenland's ice cap, early snow melt, wildlife habitat loss, destructive fires, global conflicts, disruption of agriculture, fisheries destruction, stronger and more numerous hurricanes and tornadoes, increased rainfall, droughts, ocean acidification, damage to the ocean's coral, increased insect populations, melting Arctic permafrost. It is not just the increase in heat we experience but the uncounted and still unknown changes that are now occurring to the planet that may not directly affect us yet, but they will.

Each of the above effects are occurring now and they have known and unknown multiple consequences. How is the warming of the Arctic waters changing the eco-systems of the area, the food supply for birds, fish and mammals? The polar bears are already being challenged by the lack of sea ice, what about the salmon and their need for cold water?

If things continue as they are at present certainly the world will have fiercer hurricanes, tornados, heat waves, droughts, floods and related food scarcity and health impacts. As serious as these affects are, they only predict small amount of the damage that may accelerate in the future. The damage to many eco-systems may well be irrecoverable. The very essentials of all types of life may be so disrupted that they may never be able to recover. Our oceans are heating at rates that upset the basis of life they support; essentially, they are changing and killing their own inhabitants.

Bless the young people around the world who are trying to inform us about the change in the climate. It is their future world and they have a right to be concerned.

A poem by: Warian Shire:

"Later that night

I held an Atlas in my lap

Ran my fingers across the whole world

And whispered, where does it hurt?

It answered: Everywhere, Everywhere, Everywhere"

A few examples as to what is happening to our world:
Microsoft News, The Internet, 6/9/21, Canada Launches $647 million strategy to starve off Pacific wild salmon collapse.

"Many Pacific wild salmon are on the verge of collapse, and we need to take bold action, ambitious action now if we are to reverse the trend and give them a fighting chance of survival," Fisheries Minister Bernadette Jordan said. Warming oceans due to climate change are altering the marine food web and resulting in warmer fresh water conditions pressuring salmon populations. Species such as the Chinook salmon on British Columbia's Frazer River are in steep decline and struggling to return upstream to spawning grounds each year.

June 24, 2019 Independent Record, Helena Mt., **Arctic:** Freak summertime heat across the Arctic in recent weeks has caused temperatures to soar 40 degrees F above normal and resulted in an unprecedented early melt of Greenland's ice sheet.

Arctic sea ice coverage was also at its lowest on record for mid-June. University Alaska Fairbanks scientist say they have found permafrost in Canadian Arctic is thawing 70 years earlier than predicted by computer models in yet another troubling sign that the global climate crisis is unfolding more quickly than expected. (What happens when the permafrost melts? It releases vast amounts of methane, a gas 20 times more powerful than carbon dioxide.) The Arctic heat is linked to numerous outbreaks of violent storms far to the south in North America and Europe this spring as the jet stream buckled and undulated due to the northern heat.

July 8, 2019 I.R. **Antarctic**: A new study shows Antarctica's vast ring of floating ice has undergone a sudden shift from expansion to a dramatic decline in just three years. Satellite observations show the "precipitous" disappearance of the sea ice since 2014 was greater than all of the ice lost in the Arctic during the past 34 years. "The Arctic has become a poster child for global warming," said Claire Parkinson of NASA' s Goddard Space Flight center, but scientist say the recent sea ice disappearance in Antarctic has been even greater.

July 15, 2019 USA Today, **Alaska, Bethel:** Record high temperatures are believed to be the culprit behind salmon deaths in western Alaska. Bethel based KYUK reports water temperatures on the Kuskoklum River broke into the 70's last week, the highest on record.

July 29, 2019 I.R., **Climate Consensus**: As all -time temperatures records continue to be broken in heat waves around the Northern Hemisphere this summer. Scientist say there has never been a time in the last 2000 years when global temperatures have risen so quickly. June was the hottest on record and July is likely to be the hottest as well. Scientist in three separate reports say that while the world warmed and cooled many times over the centuries, souring greenhouse gas emissions are resulting is a climate that is now warming as never before.

Aug. 20, 2019 USA Today, **Anchorage, Alaska**: The state has become America's canary in the coal mine for climate warming and the yellow bird is swooning. July was Alaska's warmest month ever according to the National Oceanic & Atmosphere Administration, 5.4 degrees above normal. Anchorage this summer had 30 days of at least 75 degrees, double the previous record.

Sept. 16, 2019, USA Today, **Pacific Ocean**: A mass of warm water extending from Baja California all the way to Alaska and the Bearing Sea could result in deaths for many sea lions and salmon as well as toxic algae blooms that can poison mussels, crabs and other sea life. The surface temperatures in the affected areas are 5 to 7 degrees above the long-range average. It covers an area of 4 million square miles or three times the size of Alaska. It's 165 to 325 deep. This event and similar events in 2014 and 2015 are not something scientist have seen before. These events coming so close together could portend a new abnormal-normal, where our old experience of what oceans look like isn't necessarily a good guide to the oceans of the future. We are fundamentally alliterating the heat balance across the whole planet.

Oct. 10, 2019, The Internet, **Rolling Blackouts**: In explaining why Pacific Gas & Electric cut power to 800,000 customers in central and northern California, Sumeet Singh, PG&E vice president for community wildfire safety programs said "extreme weather was increasing because of climate change and we do think this is a new normal that we need to be prepared for."

Nov. 4th., 2019 IR, **Rising Seas**: Global Sea rise in the deepening climate crisis, are now predicted to affect more than three times as many people by 2050 then previous models had predicted. Writing in the journal Nature Communications, researchers say that land currently home to 300 million people will flood at least once a year by mid-century due to high tides. That far exceeds the 80 million people believed to be threatened.

March 16th 2020, San Diego Union Tribune, **Alarming Melt**: Melting glaciers in Greenland and Antarctica are sending six times more water into the ocean than during the 1990's increasing sea levels more than many models had predicted. If Antarctica and Greenland continue to track the worst- case climate warming scenario, they will cause an extra 6.7 inches of sea level rise by the end of the century.

Jan. 27, 2021 USA Today. Levels of heat trapping carbon dioxide in the atmosphere today produced by the burning of fossil fuels, are higher than the earth has seen in at least 800,000 years. 2020 tied 2016 as the hottest year on record and this has been the hottest decade on record.

Jan. 28, 2021 USA Today. The stored water behind Glen Canyon Dam and Hoover Dam that service 40 million people, fed by the Colorado river are at historic lows at 37 percent.

Dog Essay's: A Dogs Prayer by Beth Norman Harris

"Treat me kindly, my beloved master, for no heart in all the world is more grateful for loving kindness then the loving heart of me.

Do not break my spirit with a stick, for though I should lick your hand between the blows, your patience and understanding will more quickly teach me the things you would have me do.

Speak to me often, for your voice is the world's sweetest music, as you must know by the fierce wagging of my tail when your footsteps fall upon my waiting ear.

When it is cold and wet, please take me inside, for I am now a domesticated animal, no longer used to bitter elements. And I ask no greater glory then the privilege of laying at your feet besides the hearth. Though had you no home, I would rather follow you through ice and snow than rest upon the softest pillow in the warmest home in all the land for you are my God and I am your devoted worshiper.

Keep my pan filled with fresh water, for although I should not reproach you were it dry, I cannot tell you when I suffer thirst. Feed me clean healthy food, that I may stay well to romp and play and do not turn me away from you. Rather hold me gently in your arms as skilled hands grant me the merciful boom of eternal rest… and I will leave you with the last breath I draw, my fate was ever safer in your hands."

Why Dogs are Smarter than Woman: Unknown Author

Dogs don't cry. Dogs love it when your friends come over. Dogs don't care if you use their shampoo. A dog's time in the bathroom is confined to a quick drink. Dogs don't expect you to call when you're running late. The later you are, the happier they are to see you. Dogs will forgive you for playing with other dogs. Dogs don't mind if you call them by another name. Dogs get excited by rough play. Dogs don't care if you give their offspring's away. Dogs understand that farts are funny. Dogs love red meat. Dogs can appreciate excessive body hair. If a dog is gorgeous other dogs don't hate it. Dogs don't shop. Dogs like it when you leave lots of things on the floor. A dog's disposition stays the same all month long. Dogs never need to examine the relationship. A dog's parents never visit. Dog love long car trips. A dog understands that instincts are better than asking for directions. Dogs like beer. Dogs don't hate their bodies. Dogs never criticize. When a dog gets old and starts to snap incessantly, you can shoot it. Dogs don't worry about germs. Dogs never expect gifts. Its legal to keep a dog chained up in your house. Dogs don't let magazine articles guide their lives. You never have to wait for a dog, they're ready to go 24 hours a day. Dogs have no use for flowers, cards or jewelry. Dogs can't talk. Dogs aren't catty. Dogs seldom outlive you. Dogs don't want to know about every other dog you ever had. Dogs like to do their own snooping outside, as opposed to your wallet, desk and the back of your sock drawer. Dogs would rather have you buy them a hamburger than a lobster for dinner. Dogs agree that you have to raise your voice to get your point across. Dogs never want foot rubs. Dogs find you amusing when you're drunk. No dog ever put on 100 pounds after reaching adulthood. My wife had the last word, "dogs don't fix dinner."

A Prince Among Dogs: By Bob Shacochis

"No canine better fits the specs of dog-ness then the Labrador Retriever, that charming, gentle blockhead who, at first glance, seems like an accessory to the woodsy folk planted in the hinterlands of Orvis catalogs. Dog and Lab melt into a single identity, an icon of harmony between man and beast. It's tempting to say there's something mechanical about the way that a Lab's fix on all things doggy-balls, sticks, chewie's, ducks-were it not for the steady exuberance they bring to the job, the always fresh flow of repetitions, which never lose their novelty in the Lab's unbounded sense of eagerness.

The game is always worth playing. The game is always fun. The ideal companion for a Lab would be a pitching machine. To a Lab work is play and play is work.

Their sense of direction is so keen they're apparently born with a GPS implanted in their quite indestructible skulls. Their dense, short coat allow them access to the marsh as well as the bedroom, although they acknowledge no limits to their territory. They're often the best, most reliable, most wholesome members of the family. Indifference is never on the Lab's menu; fidelity is, and anything that flies. They're not overly concerned with the metaphysics of existence. A Lab would make the perfect greeter at a funeral parlor: "Hi, hi, hi, how are you doing', nice to see ya, isn't this great!"

No creature on earth is better designed for the passions of both sport and love."

Remembering Today's and Yesterdays: Author Unknown

"Your furniture is covered with dog hair, and the rings if the kitchen chairs bear the marks of teething puppies.

Your car smells like kennel, and you keep moving the cocktail table around the living room to cover up stains on the rug. Your dog sleeps in the bedroom or with the kids, and the kennel is used to store the lawn mowers.

The riches people we know are dog poor. Their best investments are in memories and promises of perfect tomorrows. The pictures in your mind of Storms long retrieves or Tar's first solid point are not for sale.

Your dogs have taken you hunting, not the other way around. Days are remembered for the number of retrieves or points not the number of birds in the bag.

You're about as fond of all the silly dogs you have owned as you are of the few who turned out to be superb. You don't believe for one moment that old saying about "a man has only one good dog in a lifetime." If a man can't find something to like about almost any dog, especially his own, there's probably something wrong with the man."

The Smartest Dog; Author unknown

A group of workers were discussing how smart their dogs were. The first was an IBM worker who said his dog could do calculations. The dog was named "T-Square" and he told his dog to go to the blackboard and draw a square, a circle and triangle which the dog did with no sweat.

The Bell worker said that was good, but felt his dog was even better. His dog named "Measure" was told to get a quart of milk, pour seven ounces into a ten-ounce glass. The dog did this without any errors.

The Ford worker said he thought his dog was better. His dog, was named "Slide Rule" was told to fetch a dozen cookies and bring them back and divide into four piles of three which he did with no problem. All three workers agreed that their dogs were very smart.

Then they turned to the Civil Service worker and asked what; "What can your dog do?" The Civil Service worker then whistle shrilly and called his dog "Coffee Break." He said, show these fellows what you can do." Coffee Break went over and ate the cookies, drank the milk, screwed the other three dogs, claimed he injured his back, filed for Worker's Compensation and went home on sick leave.

A Loving Life; Dogs Have "Souls": By Chuck Wells

"I remember bringing you home. You were so small and cuddly with your tiny paws and soft fur. You bounced around the room with eyes flashing and ears flopping. Once in a while, you'd let out a little yelp just to let me know this was your territory. Making a mess of the house and chewing on everything insight became a passion, and when I scolded you, you just put your head down and looked up at me with those innocent brown eyes, as if to say, 'I'm sorry, but I'll do it again as soon as you're not watching."

As you got older, you protected me by looking out the window and barking at everyone who passed by. When I had a tough day at work, you would be waiting for me with your tail wagging, just to say: "Welcome home, I missed you." You never had a bad day; I could count on you to be there for me.

When I sat down to read the paper or watch TV, you would hop up on my lap looking for attention. You never asked for anything more then be close and have me pat your head so you could go to sleep with your head over my leg.

As you got older you moved around more slowly. Then one day old age finally took its toll, and you couldn't stand on those wobbly legs any more. I knelt down and patted you trying to make you young again. You just looked up at me as if to say that you were old and tired and after all these years of not asking for anything, you had to ask me for one favor.

With tears in my eyes, I drove you one last time to the vet. For some strange reason you were able to stand up in the animal hospital; perhaps it was your sense of pride.

As the vet led you away, you stopped for just an instant, turned your head and looked at me as if to say, "Thank you for taking care of me."

I thought, "No, thank you for taking care of me."

Stupidity:

"Scientist say that 85 % of all matter is dark matter and they don't even know what that is. Well, if it's the most abundant thing in the universe it has to be made of stupidity. Dilbert Cartoon

There are only two things in the universe that are infinite; the universe and human stupidity and I am not sure about the first." Albert Einstein

Ignorance is unfortunate. Willful ignorance is stupid.

There are two ways to be fooled. One is to believe what isn't true, the other is to refuse to believe what is true. Who is being fooled today?

Never under estimate the stupidity of the American public. For confirmation read Dear Abby.

There has always been a vaccine for "stupidity", it is called reading and thinking.

From the Sunday Comics; "Pearls Before Swine"

"Oh, great wise ass on the hill how do we rid ourselves of the pandemic that plagues us?"

"We must read more, not your face book news feed but good books that inform and enlighten, and to strive to be informed, actually informed instead of only seeking information that conforms to your world view."

And that will end covid-19? "Covd-19? I thought we were talking about stupidity." Apparently, there is more than one plague.

Are we getting smarter? A few examples.

Oct. 8, 2019 USA Today. Groom robs bank, when asked why, he said to pay for his wedding ring.

Aug. 6, 2020 Four people died and a dozen became ill after drinking hand sanitizer used for protection against the virus.

Aug. 4, USA Today. Two Delta Airline travelers refused to wear mask on a flight to Atlanta from Detroit and the plane had to turn around and return to the gate.

USA Today: Virginia, Richman. American Airlines says a flight out of Virginia was delayed after a passenger refused to comply with its policy requiring a face mask.

Oct. 8, 2020. Andrew Douglas Paige filmed himself raping a child. He received a 200- year prison sentence.

Aug. 26, 2020, Florida, Daytona Beach. A 75-year-old man who recently had heart surgery was punched in the chest and knocked down after asking a woman to maintain social distancing in a grocery store.

Arizona, Yuma: A man who was ejected from a frozen yogurt shop for not wearing a mask is facing charges for pulling out a gun in response.

Oct. 26, 2020, Idaho, Coeur d"Alene: Even as the health care situation worsened in Idaho the Panhandle Health Care District voted to repeal a local mask mandate moments after hearing how the Kootenai Hospital had reached 99% capacity. The state is experiencing its largest spike since the pandemic began, new cases increasing state-wide 46.5% over the past two weeks.

There are more of these, but you get the idea.

Remembering: Unknown author

"His eyes follow you. He joins you but still hasn't moved.
Lying outside in the yard he doesn't rise

Offering instead dozen tail thumps'
He seems to hope this is enough.
He has earned his rest

Losing your friend of the field
The memories wear deep into your own mortality
Enriching the good stuff
We lived, loved and strived a whole decade together.
Blue ribbons don't seem to matter as much anymore.

Carefully etched in time,
In yet another field or pond hundreds of miles from home
You watch him push through devastating terrain
You can't escape it, and wouldn't want to
Those were the good times that steel themselves in your mind's eye forever
Dogs wear out, you knew this when he was young but wouldn't admit it
The campaigner is tired
He leaves you snagged
On the thorns of the present by your own longevity

His final blind has been run
The last bird has been delivered
The partnership is lost in time
But the love is eternal"

Ben Franklin on Marriage: A classic from American Letters

To my dear friend: I know of no medicine to diminish the violent inclinations you mention; and if I did, I think I should not communicate it to you. Marriage is the proper remedy. It is the most natural State of Man and therefore the state in which you are most likely to find solid happiness. Your reasons against entering into it at present appear to me not well founded. The circumstantial advantages you have in view by postponing it are not only uncertain, but they are small in comparison with that of the thing itself, the being married and settled. It is the man and woman united that make the complete human being. Separate, she wants his force of body and strength of reason; he her softness, and acute discernment. Together they are more likely to succeed in the world. A single man has not nearly the value he would have in a state of union. He is an incomplete animal. He resembles the odd half of a pair of scissors. If you get a prudent, healthy wife, your industry in your profession with her good economy, will be a fortune sufficient.

But if you will not take this counsel and persist in thinking a commerce with the sex inevitable, then I repeat my former advice, that in all your amours you should prefer old woman to younger ones.

You call this a paradox and demand my reasons. They are these:

Because they have more knowledge of the world, and their minds are better stored with observations, their conversations are more importing and more lasting agreeable.

Because when woman cease to be handsome, they study to be good. To maintain their influence over men, they supply the diminution of beauty by an augmentation of utility. They learn to do a thousand services small and great and are the most tender and useful of friends when you are sick. Thus, they continue amiable. And hence there is hardly such a thing to be found as an old woman who is not a good woman.

Because there is no hazard of children, which irregularly produced may be attended with much inconvenience.

Because through more experience they are more prudent and discreet in conducting an intrigue to prevent suspicion. The commerce with them is therefore safer with regard to reputation. And with regards to theirs, if the affair should happen to be known, considerate people might be rather inclined to excuse an old woman, who would kindly take care of a young man, from his manners by good counsels, and prevent his ruining his health and fortune among mercenary prostitutes.

Because in every animal that walks upright, the deficiency of the fluids that fill the muscles appears first in the highest part. The face first grows lank and wrinkled; then the neck; then the breast and arms; the lower parts continuing to the last as plump as ever; so that covering all above with a basket, and regarding only what is below the girdle, it is impossible of two women to tell an old one from a young one. As in the dark all cats are gray; the pleasure of corporal enjoyment with an old woman's at least equal, and frequently superior every act being by practice, capable of improvement.

Because the sin is less. The debauching of a virgin may be her ruin, and make for a life unhappy.

Because the compunction is less. The having made a young girl miserable may give you frequent bitter reflection; none of which can attend the making of an old woman happy.

And lastly, they are so, grateful!

Thus, much for my paradox. But I advise you to marry directly; being sincerely your affectionate friend.
    – Ben Franklin

CPSIA information can be obtained
at www.ICGtesting.com
Printed in the USA
JSHW041725080622
26601JS00008B/22

9 781638 671558